GETTING ON TOWARD HOME

Getting on Toward Home

And Other Sermons by the River

Christoph Keller, III

Harrison Street Books

Little Rock

2021

ISBN: 978-1-7367464-0-0 (cloth)
ISBN: 978-1-7367464-1-7 (paper)
eISBN: 978-1-7367464-2-4

Designer: Rome Hernández Morgan

∞ The paper used in this publication meets the minimum requirements of the American National Standard for Permanence of Paper for Printed Library Materials Z39.48–1984

In memory of Richard Franklin Milwee
A feisty gentleman and splendid friend

He bowed his head, and the others followed his lead. Casy said solemnly, "This here ol' man jus' lived a life an' jus' died out of it. I don' know whether he was good or bad, but that don't matter much. He was alive, an' that's what matters."

—John Steinbeck, The Grapes of Wrath

Contents

Acknowledgments

This book's first readers were family members of Richard Milwee, Harry Erwin, Catherine Brown, William Terry, Virginia and Marilyn Mitchell, Christoph and Polly Keller, Naomi May, John Forster, Charles Henry, Phyllis Raney, and JJ Schreiber. I am grateful to these families for their support and trust.

I would like to thank my author friend Dr. Joanna Seibert for her encouragement and guidance; Mr. Josh Hallenbeck for his legal counsel; and Ms. Molly Bess Rector for her expert work in editing the book and guiding it to publication.

I am grateful to Kathryn Keller, my talented sister, for painting *Louisiana Reflections* and generously allowing me to show it on the cover.

Julie Keller, Christoph Keller, and Mary Olive Keller Stephens each offered helpful edits, and the occasional correction, while making me a happy man. From the bottom of my heart, I thank them.

Author's Note

This is a little book of sermons with one big thing in common: someone's death was their occasion. As could go without saying, the difference between preaching a funeral and publishing a book is enormous. In these pages I am not speaking to a roomful of mourners that includes a family in the front whose hearts are in their throats. At a funeral or memorial service there is power in the room and it reaches to the pulpit. Sometimes I fill a big cup of ice (no water, just ice) and have it in easy reach. If emotion wells up, I stop and crunch some ice. Somehow that helps me keep composure. I don't need ice to write a book.

I have given many funeral sermons. The twelve collected in this book are those that seemed to volunteer for publication; and, rather like the sorting hat at Hogwarts, they put themselves in order. Readers who start with Sermon I, for Mr. Harry Erwin, and Sermon II for Mrs. Catherine Brown (neither of whom had I ever met, though I long had known their families)—and then, as interest holds, continue down the line to Sermon XII, for young JJ Schreiber (whom I had baptized as a child)—will meet my friends and parishioners, old and new, and both my parents. I hope that when you close the book you will have seen or felt the method in the sorting.

I have done some editing for publication. Funerals happen quickly. Given extra time, when I could find a better word or phrase, I made the change. A few of those phrases ran to paragraphs.

I am a priest first, but a scholar too. You will see note numbers in the text, and find that each homily is followed by a set of endnotes. Some are scholarly, some biblical, and others anecdotal. I suggest you read a homily straight through without flipping to notes. Then, if so inclined, go back through and check the notes for sources, comment, and local color. The last sermon, on the last page, is the exception. There, you will find four footnotes at the bottom. Please read those when and as you reach them.

Introduction

My best friend in ministry was a priest named Richard Milwee. Richard and I agreed that when either of us died the other would preach his funeral. Richard went first, in 2004, so that assignment fell to me, but not before he gave instructions. Near death, Richard said, "Let's talk about your homily." I scooched my chair closer to his bed. These, verbatim, were his stipulations: "I want you to tell the truth, and nothing but the truth, but not the whole truth." Be truthful and be tactful. Those are two good rules for preaching funerals. We sat in silence for a while as I absorbed them. Then Richard quoted Augustus McRae's last words, to Woodrow Call, in *Lonesome Dove*: "It's been quite a party, ain't it?"[1] And it had.

Even as abridged for tact, the truth of Richard Milwee is a storyteller's motherlode. I told this one at the funeral. As a young candidate for ministry, Richard reported for his psychiatric evaluation, as required by the church. In our local psychiatric circles, it was still the age of Freud. After some polite warmup tosses, the psychiatrist wound up and threw the curve: "Now tell me about your sexual experience." Richard, still single in his early twenties, pondered that and let it hang, unanswered.

"Well?" the doctor insisted.

Richard: "I am not going to tell you about my sexual experience."

"And why not?" said the psychiatrist, as I imagine, leaning forward, now intrigued.

"Because I haven't had enough of it to satisfy a Freudian psychiatrist, and I've had too much to suit the church."

And that was that. In repartee, Richard never met his match. He was also strong for the right and fearless. In 1960's small-town Arkansas, Orval Faubus country, Father Milwee was a prickly advocate for racial justice. After Martin Luther King, Jr. was murdered, Richard immediately organized and publicized a community-wide service to honor him. Someone called with a warning to cancel the service: "Or else." Richard challenged the caller to come and threaten him in person if he dared. (Click.) The service went on, church-packed, I'd bet, as planned. You see my luck in having such a friend.

Rule #1: "I want you to tell the truth, and nothing but the truth." Richard's bane was pious blarney. It was foolish and faithless to pretend he must be sugar and spice and everything nice because that's what little girls and priests are made of. To so assume of any priest is foolish, because uncouth facts will giggle, belch, and peek out from underneath our vestments. People know this of their clergy and vice-versa. And pious pretense is faithless, because uncouth facts are what the gospel penetrates and heals.

Rule #2: "But not the whole truth." Richard and I agreed on two good reasons why a preacher shouldn't try to tell the truth, unvarnished, at a funeral. One, it wouldn't be polite; and two, it isn't ours to share. Omniscience is an attribute of God, not of pastors. The whole truth is for God to know and us to find out hereafter.

What people need from priests is faith to sense the compass, and the goodness, of that truth in whole. There is more to both than meets the natural eye, and at funerals it needs telling.

I buried the mother of an old friend. There was pain in the family, deep-seated, of the mother's making. Sitting around the kitchen table to discuss the service, my friend and her sister told me stories bad and good, unvarnished, trusting me (Rule #2) not to blab their family secrets. But (Rule #1) neither did they need or want to hear a made-up, pretty story of their mother from the pulpit. Their stories, the Bible, and another book or two in hand, I said my prayers and set to work. After the service, this friend of fifty years, eyes moist with relief and gratitude, and with joy mixed in, said "Chris, you made my mother beautiful." Ugly facts are not the first nor final truth about a child of God. God has seen to this in Christ. Just then my friend had seen it in her mother, whom she loves. The Holy Spirit, working through a preacher, had raised the beauty in a human life to light.[2]

I hope this gives a sense of what to look for in these pages—and find in the lives and deaths of people you hold dear.

Notes

1. Simon Wincer, director, *Lonesome Dove*, episode 4, "The Return" (CBS television mini-series adapted from the Larry McMurtry novel, first shown February 8, 1989). In conversation, Richard would assume that one knows *Lonesome Dove* as one knows Holy Scripture and the Gettysburg Address. In my case, he knew this for a fact.

2. The homily is not among the twelve included in this little volume.

I.

Harry Charles Erwin

Getting on Toward Home

January 24, 1928–February 6, 2014

The Arkansas novelist Donald Harington, a Little Rock native, whiled away his childhood summers in a tiny Ozark Mountain hamlet called Drakes Creek. From summer memories, Harington created his village of Stay More, settled in a clearing at the confluence of Banty Creek and Swains Creek, "in a narrow winding valley that snaked along through five mountains, each a thousand feet higher than the valley."[1] The town was named, people said, from the local way of taking leave. In Stay More, if you had been my guest for supper, and got up to walk home and go to bed, as host I would motion you to sit back down: "Don't be rushing off. Stay more."[2] While putting on your hat and gathering your things, you would reluctantly decline. You sure would like to stay, you would say, but had "better be gittin' on down home."[3] That was our state in days gone by.

Harry Charles Erwin grew up in those days, downstate in the small pine woodlands community of Bearden, a Ouachita County mill town. He was still young when his family moved up to Little Rock, where he would go to mighty Little Rock High School, and graduate as World War II was ending. Then, still working his way north, he moved to Fayetteville and graduated *summa cum laude* from the University of Arkansas. That requires both a good brain and a triple dose of hard work. Through an illustrious career with Russell Brown & Company, Harry helped Arkansas businesses stay on the accounting straight and narrow, in that way contributing to his native state's prosperity and growth. Tyson Foods, Allied Telephone (Alltel), Producers Rice Mill, and the First National Bank of Stuttgart all depended on him. He was a difference maker, for the good, for Arkansas.

For sixty-three years, Harry and Pat were married. To her, he was a faithful husband. To their children, Dee, Chuck, and Robert, he was a wise and loving father. As a grandfather, he was broadminded and beneficent. Come summer, Harry and Pat would round up their brood and take them far and wide to see the world.

Back in Stay More, Arkansas, lives a little girl named Latha Bourne, who finds out one day that the wider world is not much like her boxed-in, girl-sized, Ozark Mountain valley. Miss Blankinship, her teacher, passes out new geography books to students in the village's one-room school, opening for Latha a window on unimagined scenes of grandeur. Wide-eyed, she flips through pictures of cityscapes and landscapes: Baltimore, St. Louis, the Grand Canyon, Kansas wheat fields, and Egyptian pyramids. That day when the bell rings and school lets out, Latha stays back at her desk, book open, still enthralled, perplexing her friend Dorinda Whitter, who is put off by this fascination with far-flung places—missing what the scenery means to Latha. Readers misinterpret too, until Latha sets us straight. Seeing the world in pictures, she has realized that, without knowing it, "here she had been spending all her born days living in the wonderfullest place on earth."[4]

I think Harry C. Erwin might have agreed with Latha Bourne that this is a wonderful place to be from; to spread your wings and see the world from; to come home to; to marry your sweetheart and raise your family in; to draw up a chair with friends for poker in; to take grandchildren crappie fishing in—deep in Grand Prairie cypress bottoms.

There we have it: brilliant transcript, distinguished career, close-knit family, loyal friends, and a beautiful place on planet earth to love and call home. Add it all up and what do we get? A wonderful life.

What makes something wonderful?

I took that question to Thomas Aquinas. In his *Summa Theologiae*, one section has been translated as "Human Life as a Journey to God."[5] According to Aquinas, people are in most respects the same as other creatures. What sets us apart is our power to think. Along with our fellow organisms, we are attracted to some things and repulsed by others. Apple trees are drawn to goodness, so to speak, in the soil and sun or rain. A Bayou Meto bullfrog is drawn to the goodness of a well-placed lily pad, and the answering sound of an amphibian lady. Our instincts are similar. What's different is our capacity to move from an experience of goodness in things (sun, soil, rain, and lily pads) to an idea of goodness as something attractive in its own right. (People "by nature can grasp the meaning of goodness, and so be attracted to goodness as such" explains Timothy McDermott, an Aquinas scholar.)[6] "Whatever is of value, and can satisfy desire, is good," Aquinas writes, before listing three different ways that good can satisfy: "That which satisfies as a stage on the way to something else we call *useful*; that which satisfies of itself we call *worthy*, and the satisfaction found in it *delight*."[7] Delight, then, is satisfied desire, which gets us, I think, to wonderful.

Arkansas men like Harry Erwin, who hunt the woods and fish the bottoms, know deep down the meaning of delight. Harry, who so well understood the number side of doing business, often enjoyed a satisfying sense of being useful; and he was worthy, as a loving husband, friend and father.

Now, some problems: the vexation, on this journey, is that bad things shadow good; the sorrow, on this journey, is that good things come and go. Aquinas knew that life is only episodically delightful. "We can be partially happy in this life," he warned, "but not completely and truly. For there are many ills that cannot be avoided in this life: ignorance of mind, unbalanced attachments, all sorts of bodily pains. And we also naturally desire the good things we have to last whereas in this life they pass away. Indeed life itself passes away, though by nature we desire it and wish it to last and shrink from death."[8] The purely wonderful life lies over the horizon.

Now, another question: Over that horizon, what awaits?

Our faith tells us this much. It won't feel, for anyone, as much like getting a diploma, *summa cum laude*—due reward for work exceptionally well done—as like waking up at home in Bearden, Arkansas, five years old, on Christmas morning. Eyes pop open knowing *yes! today's the day*. This is a gift and pure delight.

Faith knows the giver is God, through Christ, and it remembers that for him, the giving wasn't easy. This resonates. As givers ourselves, we find that love is sometimes painful, and appreciate that we and God have that experience in common. When we see God face to face, we won't meet him as a stranger.

Isaiah foretells a mountain feast for all the peoples, "of rich food filled with marrow, of well-aged wines strained clear."[9] If Isaiah hailed from Bearden, he might have seen this as a lowland crappie-season fish fry, with beer on ice. Either way one takes the point, that goodness as we know it here and now draws us on toward higher goodness there and then—like delicious smells wafting from the kitchen. St. Paul suggests a comparison of tents and houses. "For we know that if the earthly tent we live in is destroyed, we have . . . a house not made with hands, eternal in the heavens."[10] He is talking about souls and bodies. We know tents as flimsy, and well-built houses as secure. By analogy, we can roughly estimate the expected change from life now to life "eternal in the heavens." We can imagine Harry Erwin now altered, to the good, by that close-enough-for-horse-shoes measure. You would know him when you saw him, but would be amazed, delighted. At your meeting, when it comes, his amazed delight on seeing you will mirror yours.

Aquinas is so right. We shrink from death. Our nature is to hate and fear it. When those we love draw near to death, our every fiber strains to keep them with us. We want them to stay more. Today we grieve the loss of this accomplished human being. But, in grief, we made it out to church, this icy winter morning, also to reckon with the fact that there was always more to him than nature, by its own devices, could account for; and to embrace the gospel truth that, from Bearden, Arkansas on January 24, 1928, to Little Rock on February 6, five days ago, Harry Charles Erwin was on a journey to God—and for him, the time had come for getting on toward home.

Notes

1. Donald Harington, *The Architecture of the Arkansas Ozarks* (New York: Harvest/HBJ, 1975), 4.

2. For example, see: Donald Harington, *Lightning Bug* (New York: Harvest/HBJ, 1970), 3.

3. Donald Harington, *The Choiring of the Trees* (New York: Harvest/HBJ, 1991), 371.

4. Donald Harington, *Enduring* (New Milford, CT: Toby, 2009), 72.

5. Timothy McDermott, ed. and trans, *St. Thomas Aquinas: Summa Theologiae, A Concise Translation* (Notre Dame, IN: Christian Classics / Ave Maria Press, 1989). This is Timothy McDermott's lay-friendly recasting of the *Summa Theologiae* in prose form, stripped of Aquinas's rigorous methodological procedure. McDermott's seventh chapter is titled "Human Life as a Journey to God."

6. McDermott, *Summa: Concise Translation*, 167.

7. McDermott, 168.

8. McDermott, 181.

9. Isa. 25:6. Except where otherwise indicated, scriptural citations are to the New Revised Standard Version of the Bible (NRSV).

10. 2 Cor. 5:1.

II.

Catherine Fuller Porter

Brown

Where Is Boots?

July 13, 1919–February 20, 2019

Catherine Fuller Porter Brown—"Boots" to her friends, Mrs. Brown to me—was born in the deep south and died on the Pacific coast,[1] which reminds me of something Thomas Wolfe said about provincialism. As I remember, it went like this: west coasters aren't provincial; mid-westerners are provincial and ashamed of it; southerners are provincial and proud of it; and northeasterners are provincial and don't know it.[2] Even after more than a decade of life on Puget Sound, I doubt we could find as much as a drop of the west coast in the soul of Mrs. Brown. Marianna, Arkansas had been too small, but Seattle too north and too west, to her taste. Memphis in its heyday (where she grew up) suited her just fine.

She had a facility with French, loved to read novels, and raised a daughter who developed a lifelong love of Proust. I spent some time with Proust early in my ministry, and for a pastor it was time well spent. Proust knew the human heart, where good and mischief coexist. Heart and mind, conscious and subliminal, are the theater of action in his masterpiece, *In Remembrance of Things Past*, in which he portrays what he called "states of soul." The novel has no plot because the author saw in these transient states "something not . . . less serious than the events of everyday life but, on the contrary, so far superior to it as to be alone worth while expressing."[3] The scenery is sometimes scary. Proust was well attuned to dark shadows concealed by sunny pious sentiments.

Proust viewed the body as a temple, as had the Apostle Paul.[4] He recognized and valued archetypes, as would Carl Jung. Proust called these "the rich possessions wherewith our inner temple is diversified and adorned."[5] Although we can be no more than partially aware of these possessions, we have intimations of them through buried memories—unearthed by old songs and favorite smells. Glen Miller on the radio could take Boots back to Memphis reveries, I'd bet. Maybe Elvis would reach her too, though of that I'm not so sure.

Our states of soul are flavored by place and time, which for Boots meant prewar, pre–Brown v. Board of Education, big band, King Cotton Memphis. Ninety-nine years old, she knew, as we do not, what it was to live through a war we could well have lost and had to win. She knew, and most of us here do too, what it was to have one's way of life surrender to a greater good. Boots looked on as her daughter grew up into a world where doors that had been locked for her began cracking open—representing opportunities almost unthinkable. She saw that daughter seize her chances and pave her way by work, talent, and ambition. She lived to see her unprovincial grandchildren, full of gumption, out of the starting gate, off and running into a new century—a future fraught with peril and full of possibility, just as hers had been as she was growing up in Memphis. In their memories and DNA, she now lives on—a trace of old south spice in west coast souls. Proudly, I say that flavor is a plus.

As Proust paints them, our souls teem with such riches, personified as "hostages . . . divine captives who will follow and share our fate." And there's the rub. As they live in us, so their lives depend on ours, and when we expire, they die. Ever the romantic, Proust finds consolation: "Death in their company is somehow less bitter, less inglorious," he muses—then adds, in an oddly written afterthought that moves beyond romance into something more, "perhaps even less probable."[6] Unless I am mistaken, here Proust is on the cusp of faith.

Last Saturday afternoon, my son sent along a *New York Times* Easter Sunday edition interview, just released online, asking for comment.[7] The respondent is the Rev. Dr. Serene Jones, President of Union Seminary in New York. For the *Times,* Nicholas Kristof asks Dr. Jones for thoughts about the resurrection: "Happy Easter Reverend Jones! To start, do you think of Easter as a literal flesh–and–blood resurrection? I have problems with that." Her answer is agnostic. "Those who claim to know whether it happened or not are kidding themselves," she replies. "But that empty tomb symbolizes that the ultimate love in our lives cannot be crucified and killed." Kristof follows up: "What happens when we die?" Again, the answer is agnostic. "I don't know!" she exclaims. "There may be something, there may be nothing. My faith is not tied to some divine promise about the afterlife."

My faith is. My faith is tied both to the resurrection of Jesus from the dead, I am speaking literally, and the promise of the afterlife. (So is my belief, shared with Dr. Jones, that the ultimate love in our lives will finally prevail—though obviously it can be killed, and even crucified.) As a pastor, I pray I have always made this clear.[8]

First came Friday and the death of Jesus Christ. I imagine Jesus in his grave. I think of those rich possessions of his temple, hostage states of soul, entombed. Down into the grave they went: memories of Martha, Lazarus, and the several Marys, with the woman of Samaria and the man born blind; down went Jesus' songs, loves, compassion—his integrity and courage in the face of opposition; down into the tomb went all remembrance of things past, good times and bad. Down perhaps went thoughts—possibly regrets—of marriage and children: his road not taken. Down into darkness went the power that had rendered broken men and women whole; and down, his unique sense of God as intimate and ready. God the Holy Spirit was the inmost treasure Jesus carried down into his grave.

Then came Sunday morning. From the vacant tomb, Mary Magdalene ran back and announced to the disciples: "I have seen the Lord."[9]

What had happened?

Within the soul of Jesus, beautifully adorned, was the rich possession (divine, but not captive) death could neither fathom nor contain. God abided with his Son: secretly persisting with him on the cross, when apparently forsaken; descending with him into total darkness; dwelling there, intimate and ready, as love among the ruins.[10] On the third day, God Almighty stirred him, his treasure stock of memories and loves intact, to life. That Easter Sunday, God unlatched the door into eternity, through which Christ leads us on our way, exultant.

What happens when we die?

We live.

Where is Boots?

Across the river.

Notes

1. Catherine and her husband had moved in 2003 from Little Rock to Seattle, to be near their daughter and her family. When the time came, they wanted her to take them both back home for burial. They asked that their ashes be committed to the Arkansas River. Catherine's service of committal (and this homily) took place in Little Rock on Thursday in Easter Week, April 25, 2019, on the riverbank at Little Rock, with giant thunderstorms rolling in—an archetypal April day in Arkansas.

2. My recollection was imperfect and had reworked Wolfe's southerner's lament into a quip. What he actually wrote: "New England is provincial and doesn't know it, the Middle West is provincial, and knows it, and is ashamed of it, but, God help us, the South is provincial, knows it, and doesn't care." Thomas Clayton Wolfe, unpublished note, quoted in John Shelton Reed, *One South: An Ethnic Approach to Regional Culture* (Baton Rouge, LA: Louisiana State University Press, 1982), 157.

3. Marcel Proust, *In Search of Lost Time: The Complete Masterpiece*, rev. ed., trans. C. K. Scott Moncrieff, Terence Kilmartin, and Andreas Mayor, rev. D. J. Enright, vol. 1, *Swann's Way* (New York: Modern Library, 1992), loc. 6536 of 56137, Kindle.

4. 1 Cor. 3:17: "God's temple is holy, and you are that temple."

5. Proust, *Swann's Way*, loc. 6564.

6. Proust, loc. 6574.

7. Nicholas Kristof, "Reverend, You Say the Virgin Birth Is 'a Bizarre Claim'?" *New York Times*, April 20, 2019.

8. As clear as Karl Barth was, I hope, when he averred that if Jesus has not "visibly and corporally" risen from the dead, then "the whole Christian church is based on an illusion and the whole of what is called Christianity is one huge piece of moral sentimentalism, to which we cannot say farewell soon enough." Karl Barth, *The Knowledge of God and the Service of God According to the Teaching of the Reformation*, The Gifford Lectures for 1937–38, trans. J.L.M. Haire and Ian Henderson

(Eugene, OR: Wipf and Stock, 1938), 87, https://books.google.com/
books/about/The_Knowledge_of_God_and_the_Service_of.htm-
l?id=hYNLAwAAQBAJ.

9. John 20:18.

10. This is an allusion to another favorite novel, Walker Percy's *Love
in the Ruins.*

III.

William Leake Terry

"V"

October 11, 1922–December 25, 2016

For some of us, *The Crown* was must-see television this fall.[1] It tells the story of England's Elizabeth II as a girl and young queen. *The Crown* is soulful like *Friday Night Lights* and dressed up like *Downton Abbey*. Episode seven is titled "Scientia Potentia Est" (Knowledge is Power).[2] We find that Elizabeth is embarrassed by her lack of learning. She feels the lack most keenly in her weekly chats with Winston Churchill, her prime minister, whose talk is salted and peppered with philosophy and history. It is not her fault that (relative to Churchill) she is ignorant. Elizabeth had been home schooled by palace tutors, who spent hours upon hours drilling her on protocol and etiquette: who sat where and talked to whom when entertaining heads of state. The one tidbit of philosophy they taught her was a silly-seeming distinction between "dignified" and "efficient" components of the English Constitution. This was a play on Aristotle's four causes: material, formal, efficient, and final. Elizabeth was instructed that, as queen, the dignified, symbolic power would be hers. The efficient power was the political machinery through which laws were made and things actually got done. That now belonged to Churchill. Watching from my couch, I think: the crown and a quarter buys a cup of coffee. Then, as the episode unfolds, we come to a moment dangerous for England, when it takes the queen's shrewd exercise of dignity to save the day. With Elizabeth, we realize that her peculiar homeschooled knowledge could be potent, and that her royal dignity is too.

William L. Terry was born with dignity. He bore it naturally, humbly, and heroically. It was for someone like Bill that the epitaph was coined:

He bore an honored name, but what is more,
He added honor to the name he bore.[3]

A congressman's son from Arkansas, a quiet boy, he rose to the top of the ranks at St. Alban's School as senior prefect. He rowed crew at Princeton. Pearl Harbor came December 7 of his freshman year. Although he hadn't yet graduated, he enlisted. He wanted to fly but was informed he was too tall. The army later let him serve as a gunner on B-17 bombers only because he fibbed about his height. He completed thirty-four missions over Europe. From the start, he knew the odds of his surviving that were small.

I was ordained in 1982, at which time the World War II airmen were beginning to retire. They were still vigorous: one of my first senior wardens had been a bomber pilot in the European theater, and when he wasn't playing golf, he was up and down the Ozark ridges hunting quail. I went back for his funeral six years ago. It has now been seventy-five years since Pearl Harbor. Bill's comrades in arms who still survive cope as best they can with ravages of time. In *The Crown*, we see Churchill struggling with indignities of advancing years, including his need to sit down in the queen's presence. Nor has Elizabeth herself, in real life, been spared: this Christmas Day she wasn't feeling up to attending church. Death and infirmity are no respecters of dignity in monarchs, prime ministers, or heroic generations. This is the downslope Paul alludes to in his epistle: "What is sown is perishable, what is raised is imperishable. It is sown in dishonor, it is raised in glory. It is sown in weakness, it is raised in power."[4] The downslope comes with human nature, as the antithesis of glory.

Bill was dutiful son to a famous and imposing mother, Adolphine Fletcher Terry.[5] At her urging, he kept a diary of his military service: "William L. Terry: Diary of Overseas Service with 388th Bomb Group, 560th Bomb Squadron, Eighth Air Force, England, March–August, 1944."[6] The first entry was made stateside, while he was still in training.

> February 26, 1944: Called home tonight after the Prisoner of War lecture. Mom said to be sure and keep a diary, something I've always shied from, so here goes. Here's hoping this lasts more than a week.

Skipping forward and across the Atlantic, here is an entry from his second mission:

> March 28: Mission #2 (8 ½ hours) Boy we hated to get up at 3:00 ... bombed airfield at Bordeaux .... Long trip. Heavy flak. Hit in several places. Bomb rack from another plane lodged in wing. #2 engine cut out over target and we had to drop out of formation and lose our altitude. Not too pleasant to be that far from home and all by yourself.

For excitement, that run was about average.

A result of this sort of work would be that democracy was saved on both sides of the Atlantic, and life could return to normal. That was the point of winning—that life as we have known it could happen; that life as Adolph Hitler would have had us live it did not occur. In a September 8, 1941 essay for *Time* magazine, a great Swiss/German theologian named Karl Barth asked England and America to declare war on his own country to prevent Hitler from forcing his new order on the world. Barth was blunt: "We Christians do not accept this war as a necessary evil. We approve it as a righteous war, which God commands us to wage ardently."[7]

With valor and distinction, Bill Terry did his part to win that war. Then he came home to court his girl, Betty Kilbury. His friend and neighbor Sanford McDonnell, who would go on to run McDonnell Douglas Corporation, urged him on. Sandy called Betty "Betty Boop," and "Boop" for short. Bill and Boop would have a knack for making daughters.[8]

And life in the free world rolled on. Money and laws were made. Novels and songs were written. Gizmos and gadgets were invented. Men flew on rockets to the moon. Elections were held and Republicans and Democrats took turns in office. Crises were faced, including the notorious one in Little Rock, in which Bill and his mother both played parts.[9] Smaller wars were won and lost; as were football games that felt like wars. After football season, blinds were brushed so that, come winter, Bill and his friends could drive down to Arkansas County, to their tents at Tuf Nut, to drink and talk football and politics by night around the campfire, sleep warm in massive sleeping bags, then get up and out before daybreak to be ready when wood ducks zoomed by and mallards dropped into flooded timber.[10] When wives and daughters came down, the men could dress camp up a bit and shake the mice out of the sleeping bags—or maybe not.

If you were Bill, you had won the war so things like that could happen—and things like Brown v. Board of Education, and the dawn of civil rights for black folks, who had also fought against the Nazis. And so you could take your daughters out to Barton Coliseum to see the youthful, handsome president of the United States, hoisting your youngest to your shoulders for a better look.[11] And in springtime, you and your buddies and could drive your families up into the Ozarks on Highway 7, then drop down to the low water bridge at Ponca to float the prettiest river in America,[12] spending a night riverside at Camp Orr, where you could laugh around the campfire about who got tumped and how at Gray Rock. And in summer, you could pull your girls up on water skis and run them up and down the lake at Scott, telling them not to mind the cottonmouths: "They're more scared of you than you are of them," which they knew was propaganda. But you had beaten Hitler so you could say that, do that, and they could roll their eyes, and laugh, and love you for it. And they could grow up and get married, or not, and have children of their own—two girls, one boy—and you could dote on them, take pride in them, and send them back east to college: Wellesley, Vassar, and Princeton, taking joy in that. And you could show them, yourself, that dignity is power—proving that by your effect on them, and on your friends, your church, and your law firm. And you could do all that honorably, humbly, quietly—because all your life you could be that kind of man.

July 14: Mission #29 (after D-Day): The best mission yet, a secret one, dropping supplies to the French patriots in the mountains below Bordeaux. Really a long run. Off at 3:30 and over the invasion coast, my first real look at it. Millions of ships all along. Clouds then covered up all northern France . . . Let down and by the time we reached the i.p. we were at 500 feet. Saw people waving etc., really fun. Big bonfires directed the planes [to the drop]. Circled a few times and then flew back gaining altitude all the way. Fighters were in the vicinity but didn't attack us, thank God.

By end of August, Bill had completed his missions. He

boarded the Queen Mary, doing duty as a troop ship through the war, for the voyage home: destination New York, with a stop in Halifax, Nova Scotia. Before departure, the ship lingered overnight in port, giving rise to rumors.

August 30: Eleven of us are in one stateroom on canvas 3 decker bunks that really make a racket when you turn over.

September 1: Still in port: Big rumor is that Churchill is coming aboard.

September 10: Arrival in North America: Big Day! Went up on the boat deck to be sure and see everything . . . . Canadian Mounties were all over the place keeping the people away. Finally the bunch steamed down the gangway, admirals, WRNS, WAAFS, etc. Then after a pause Mrs. Churchill came out and after her the old boy, smoking the biggest cigar I ever saw. Then after they were in the shed a little while meeting the committee, they came back out and waved to us for a little while and gave the V sign.

Through the bravery and sacrifice of men like William L. Terry, the efficient powers of democracy and decency, prevailed.

And now for Bill something comparable occurs. "The last enemy to be destroyed is death."[13] The resurrection of the dead is pure divine efficient power. It happens because God is able and willing to make it so. Why would God want to raise the dead? We wonder with the psalmist: "What are human beings, that you are mindful of them?"[14] Consider the abiding love of Bill for Boop; their daughters Beth, Ellen, and Susan; their granddaughters Eliza and Rachael; and their grandson Fletcher. What would he not do for them if he could do it? Would he raise them from the dead? He would and no one doubts it. What I say next is said in faith. Christmas, the day Bill Terry died, is the basis for it. God's love isn't less than Bill's—it is more. As the brightness of the moon reflects the (unseen) splendor of the sun, so is a human father's love a reflection of its source in God.

I borrow the analogy from Paul's: "There is one glory of the sun, and another glory of the moon." [15] Paul's suggests the great illumination that occurs through death and res-urrection. Life now is moonlit by comparison. Then Paul intensifies his point by switching metaphors. Moving from moonlight–sunlight difference of degree, to dramatic death–life change in kind, he drives home the resurrection gospel: "What is sown is perishable, what is raised is imperishable. It is sown in dishonor, it is raised in glory. It is sown in weak-ness, it is raised in power." [16] Here is our promise of human dignity retained, restored, and magnified in life to come, through the loving efficiency of God.

So be it.

Notes

1. This was the fall of 2016, the first season.

2. *The Crown*, season 1, episode 7, "Scientia Potentia Est," directed by Benjamin Caron, written by Peter Morgan, featuring Claire Foy, released Nov. 4, 2016, on Netflix, https://www.netflix.com/watch/80025763?trackId=200257859.

3. Francis T.P. Plimpton, quoted in Ted Lamont, *The Happiness of the Pursuit: Felicitous Episodes along the Way* (New York: Hamilton Books / Rowman and Littlefield, 2006), 277, https://books.google.com/books/about/The⬜Happiness⬜of⬜the⬜Pursuit.html?id=pH7caT1I7EoC.

4. 1 Cor. 15:42–43.

5. Adolphine Fletcher Terry is an Arkansas legend, best remembered for having founded and vigorously led the Women's Emergency Committee to Open Our Schools in 1958, after Little Rock public high schools were closed in defiance of racial desegregation.

6. William L. Terry, "Diary of Overseas Service with 388th Bomb Group, 560th Bomb Squadron, Eighth Air Force, England, March-August, 1944," unpublished private diary. When, the day after Christmas, I went by to visit Betty Terry and her daughters, Betty handed me the diary and said "You might want to have a look at this." Rapt, I read it cover to cover that day.

7. "Karl Barth Declares War," *Time*, September 8, 1941, 43. Barth was born in Basel, Switzerland and remained a Swiss citizen. He studied and taught in Germany for many years. He was expelled, in 1935, for refusing to sign an oath of allegiance to Adolph Hitler.

8. They raised three—and no sons.

9. The Little Rock Central High School desegregation crisis of 1957.

10. Tuf Nut Hunting Club in Gillette, Arkansas, is perhaps the most renowned, and certainly the most rustic, of historic Arkansas flooded timber duck camps. To this day, hunters sleep in army surplus tents, warmed by wood stoves.

11. President John F. Kennedy spoke in Little Rock on October 3, 1963, on his way to the dedication of Greer's Ferry Dam in Heber Springs—his last public appearance outside Washington before the trip to Dallas: November 22, 1963.

12. The Buffalo River.

13. 1 Cor. 15:26.

14. Ps. 8:4.

15. 1 Cor. 15:41.

16. 1 Cor. 15:42–43.

IV.

Virginia Grobmyer Mitchell

Changed, Not Ended

November 24, 1913–February 19, 2005

I don't know what you were doing last week, but I can tell you what Virginia Mitchell was up to. She was reading a book by Charlie May Simon about Pierre Teilhard de Chardin.[1] Teilhard was that French paleontologist and theologian, in whose thought a scientific account of the evolution of life on earth could seamlessly blend with a theological understanding of the origin, significance, and destiny of humankind—in his words: "the phenomenon of man." To realize that this sort of food for thought was on Virginia's plate, up to the last week of her life, is to feel a little sheepish, as I reflect on some hours in my life spent watching the *World Series of Poker* from Binion's Horseshoe, and *Petticoat Junction* reruns.

Question: Who didn't love Virginia Mitchell?
Answer: No one!

My morning assignment is not, however, to the add to the true good news of Virginia Mitchell, some of which we've sampled in this service from the hearts of people she held dear. My charge is to recall a promise Virginia knew and treasured, that death is "swallowed up" in victory.[2] The words are St. Paul's. How many times in her ninety-one years did Virginia sit in the nave of this cathedral, as you sit now, in grief or with respect for a friend, loved one, or acquaintance, and hear that death-defying proclamation? Guessing,

I will put the number in the hundreds, while sharing my observation that, more than many, Virginia took the words to heart.

"Death is swallowed up in victory."

When you come to a Christian church for a service of this sort, we surround you with symbols, songs, and words of hope. This hope, put simply, is that when we die our lives are changed, not ended. Naturally, a suspicion arises that this is only wishful thinking. We feed our hope with the story of a young man who lived and died some time ago—a long time, according to our usual reckoning; although, to one who has been absorbing Teilhard de Chardin, it might seem like only yesterday. You well know the story and man I have in mind. He was denied the long, full life and peaceful death that we aspire to, and so desperately want for those we love. That we would look to him, a life cut short, for hope, is striking. Hope starts where hope seemed lost.

You also know, and I do too, that there are people who face death with hopes that don't have much, or anything, to do with Jesus. There were religions and philosophies that regarded death in hope before he came along; there are religions, and surely still at least a philosophy or two, that do so now. These hopes are a kaleidoscope of shifting images and colors, with promises that range from awful or insipid to sublime. Shake the tube once and see those seventy-two virgins we've heard much of lately. Shake it again and find the pure land of Mahayana Buddhist expectation, and its Christ-like savior figure. An Indian prince named Dharmakara was an enlightened bodhisattva, who postponed his entrance to nirvana for the sake of unenlightened multitudes. For them, he created a waystation, the pure land—a climate friendly to spiritual achievement, in contrast to our coarse world of politics and poker, attachment to friends and family, and desire for sex and money. In the pure land, the undistracted soul is finally free to give the spirit its complete attention.[3] Like Jesus in John 14, Dharmakara had gone ahead to pre- pare a place for his disciples, that where he was, they could be also. Karl Barth called Pure Land Buddhism the most "comprehensive and illuminating" non-Christian parallel he knew of to the gospel.[4]

Christians' hopes are kaleidoscopic too, and wide-rang- ing. (As wide as the difference, let's say, between an evening in a stuffed chair reading Teilhard, and a night at the drive- in watching *Left Behind*.) In our vicinity, the woods are dot- ted with churches whose hope isn't wide enough to include Episcopalians. Not even Virginia Mitchell, the very soul of Christian kindness, is eligible for heaven. That absurdi- ty reminds me of a friendly, big-church Crawford County preacher (Assemblies of God), who told me once over lunch that the only kind of Christian he had no use for was the one who wouldn't let him go to heaven with him. We shook hands on that.

I doubt that many here are bothered much by narrow or exotic hopes in other churches or religions. Our menace is oblivion. People underestimate the atmospheric weight we shoulder, day to day, from mortal fear of our extinction and of final separation from our loved ones. My family of four lived in New York City on 9-11. As parents in the after- math, Julie and I were concerned about another terrorist scenario, and what might happen to our children. Now, as parents right here in River City, we may worry even more, on Friday nights, as our high school daughter ventures out to God knows where, full car, sophomore driver at the wheel. Through war and peace this threat is present. In the grand evolutionary scheme, our worry with it is no doubt a useful adaptation, a fit to our environment, beneficial to survival. But it takes a toll: mental, emotional, and spiritual. The biblical writers, toll-payers, describe it as death's "shadow" and its "sting," as in: "Yea though I walk through the valley" of its shadow;[5] and: "O death, where is thy sting?"[6]

Virginia's peaceful death, closing out her long, full life, will not for most of us be difficult to bear. It leaves a gentle hurt ("sweet sorrow") to season happy memories and gratitude. For some here closest to her, though, her loss could be an ordeal.[7] Through the course of her own life, Virginia was well acquainted with death's sting and shadow—including being worried sick over Jim, her son, through his dangerous tour in Vietnam. I've been told more than once the story of Bishop Keller's going to the Mitchell house on one tense night, during battle, to sit with Will and Virginia, wait for word on Jim, and pray. Will died in 1981, and she didn't stop missing him from then until last Saturday.

With such sad facts (and worse) in mind, St. Paul drew his memorable line in the sand regarding resurrection: "If for this life only we have hoped in Christ, we are of all people most to be pitied."[8] Paul said this only to emphasize that such is not the case. He did not doubt that, here on the mark where Christian faith would stand or fall, it stands. Our hope in Christ for this life is only the beginning. Life is changed, not ended. Death is swallowed up in victory. It may be no exaggeration to say that, on the strength of his encounter with the risen Christ, for Paul the sting of death was gone.

Virginia wrote recently about her first and fondest hope for heaven: to see Will again. To that I say right on. Hope blesses love's longing for reunions. The imagination tries hard, but I doubt it can be of much use in picturing these meetings. I say this not because our imagination wants to promise too much and reach too high (or low), but because, stretch as it may, human imagination is obviously no match for God's. Can rocks imagine movies? Rock brains may be better equipped for that work than ours are to concoct a day in life across the river—until, that is, our imagination too is changed.

Virginia Mitchell's life is changed (not ended). Death's shadow and sting are *left behind*. Heart, mind, imagination all evolve to fit their new environment: the unveiled truth of God—

Her Joy.

Her Life.

Her All.

Notes

1. Charlie May Hogue Simon, *Faith Has Need of all the Truth: A Life of Pierre Teilhard de Chardin* (New York: Dutton, 1974.) On his election night, President Bill Clinton described Arkansas as "this small, wonderful state." To that point: Charlie May Simon's husband was the poet John Gould Fletcher; whose sister was Adolphine Fletcher Terry; whose son was William Leake Terry, whose funeral homily you will have read preceding this one.

2. 1 Cor. 15:54 (King James Version).

3. John B. Cobb, Jr., *Beyond Dialogue: Toward a Mutual Transformation of Christianity and Buddhism* (Philadelphia: Fortress Press, 1982), 122–26.

4. Karl Barth, *Church Dogmatics* I.2, ed. G.W. Bromiley and T.F. Torrance, trans. G. T. Thomson and Harold Knight (Edinburgh: T. & T Clark,1956), 340.

5. Ps. 23:4 (KJV).

6. 1 Cor. 15:55 (KJV).

7. In saying this I had one person especially in mind: Virginia's adult daughter Marilyn, who lived with her at home. Marilyn would die eleven years later, and, in this book, her funeral homily is next.

8. 1 Cor. 15:19.

V.

Marilyn Elizabeth Mitchell

Hers for the Taking

July 3, 1956–June 10, 2016

Marilyn Mitchell was a friend of mine, and for as long as I have known her, she has struggled. That is a long time, going back almost to when I moved to Little Rock in 1967. At Central High School, we were classmates.[1] Her parents, William and Virginia, were dear friends to mine. I buried (and treasured) Virginia. Both the Mitchell and Keller clans were closely knit and fully stocked with decent, interesting, and accomplished people. Marilyn was one such, but playing with a tougher hand. Life is not fair at all. Through no fault of her own, Marilyn was overtaken as a girl by a devilish affliction. In the old days it would have been said she was tormented by demons, as were many who sought help from Jesus. Today, and this is an improvement, we call the condition mental illness. Judging from the Bible, Jesus was better at curing it than we are.

Of all illnesses, mental ones are the worst, in my opinion, because they disable the spirit as they aggrieve the body. We can spiritually equip ourselves (I think) to cope with cancer. With schizophrenia, our coping equipment has gone haywire. One suffers through, and family and friends are left to do the coping.

Kellers have suffered mental torments too, including two of the most decent, interesting, and accomplished of us. I have in mind my father, the bishop,[2] whose descent into Alzheimer's disease was a ten-year nightmare for him and for his family. I am also remembering my brother-in-law Robin

Gilliland. When word came last week that Marilyn had been diagnosed with a glioblastoma, I shuddered and thought immediately of Robin. "Glioblastoma": even the word is sinister. It is a brain tumor, malignant and aggressive. Robin died from his in December, 1980. The tumor had attacked and cut him down in the prime of life. He was thirty-nine years old, with two young children at home and his wife, my sister Caroline, pregnant, when the radiologist reported out the dreaded diagnosis. Robin bravely held his poise, and for the most part kept his wits, as the disease advanced, but he suffered from hallucinations, including one with flying pigs that he could paint as comic. Marilyn's worst hallucinations were not funny on any telling. Her tribulations started early and lasted long. As painful as their illnesses were for Robin and my father, Marilyn had the harder row to hoe by far.

Marilyn persevered. She had friends. She had skills. She had dogs. She was smart and quick-witted. She understood money and was careful with it. There was a man she loved. Courageously, against intimidating odds, she earned her bachelor's degree. Along with those virtues of prudence, fortitude, and perseverance, she was also faithful and hopeful—ready to give God the glory.

Theology is "faith seeking understanding." Evil, I do not fully understand—far from it. As a theologian that puts me in good company. Daniel Migliore—whose book *Faith Seeking Understanding* includes a thorough introduction to the problem—warns readers: "Our effort to relate our faith in God to the brutal facts of life leads into a labyrinth of unanswered questions."[3] Among the greatest Christian thinkers, Thomas Aquinas and Karl Barth can be insightful on the topic because they don't pretend to solve the riddle. Aquinas's search for understanding led to an unexpected diagnosis: evil is a parasite on good. (The Latin term is *privatio boni*.)[4] If all good were eliminated from creation, all evil would vanish with it.[5] The flip side isn't true. If all evil were removed, much of creation would remain, and all of it good. A second insight: in that case, however, some good things would be lost. Courage is an obvious example. Beyond that, there is not a lot that we can say for sure. A little faith is enough to accept that as humans we are organisms, not machines; that with that condition come incessant travail, marvelous delights, and agonizing problems; and that, as hill folk sing at funerals, we'll understand it better by and by.

In November 1980, twenty-nine days before Robin died, I preached for the first time. It was at little Christ Church, in the Hyde Park neighborhood of Boston. I was in my "middler" (second) year of seminary and Christ Church was my field education placement. Robin now had been sick for about a year. His new son, Robin, was three months old.

The gospel reading appointed for that Sunday was Luke 20:27–38, which begins: "Some Sadducees, those who say there is no resurrection, came to him" (that is, to Jesus) "and asked him a question." The question was meant only to trip him up, and we can save it for another day. In Luke, it sparks a debate as to whether death is final for the faithful. The Sadducees stand on their belief that death means annihilation. Jesus argues it does not. The Lord "is God not of the dead, but of the living." With dying Robin on my mind, and that assurance hanging in the Sunday morning air above the pews, I put the point at issue to the congregation. "Do you believe in heaven?" Before thumbs could go up or down, I showed my cards. "I do," I announced, and told them why I felt that was important:

Christians have been ridiculed, and rightly so, for talking of heaven as a way of getting around the suffering and injustice that often come with life. "Pie in the sky in the sweet by and by" is what critics say we offer, and I do not want to give the impression that I feel that this is what Christianity is all about. Many do suggest, carelessly, when people are hurting, that it shouldn't matter, or that it matters less—because everything will be all right in heaven. It does matter. You know that it matters and how much. But it would be wrong to replace over-emphasis on heaven with silence about life after death with God. Hope for heaven isn't frill and lace for Christian faith—it is woven in its fabric. We need to hope for heaven. And why is that? Because there is a problem—we all know this—with life on earth. We suffer here, in a lot of ways, including pain from sickness and the approach of death. There is injustice, including to children born in families that cannot give them love, who grow up not knowing love at all, and may die that way too. Then there is the opposite problem. The rest of us need to hope that death is not final because we build relationships with people we love. They fill our lives with meaning, so we do our best to foster them. But we find that all these relationships lead eventually to partings—including, in every case, a final one. What we build up is torn down. On earth, even our relationship with God is incomplete. That is why people through every age of history have looked to death not only with fear of annihilation, but with hope that death might open upon a fuller, richer life than we have now.[6]

The sermon went on . . . and on. (My first sermon may have been my longest.) You see the point. That day, along with Robin, I had Marilyn in mind. She represented something to me then, and she still does. It was wrong that she should know such pain. What I said before, I still maintain. Our lives on earth are unfinished business. I refuse to accept, and do not believe, that it is for this life only that we have hoped in Christ.[7] I choose to accept, and do in fact believe, that the beautiful and marvelous potential that was Marilyn Elizabeth, beloved daughter of William and Virginia, is hers for the taking now.

Notes

1. We were classmates in the sense that we took a class or two together. Looking at the yearbook, I am reminded that I was a year ahead of Marilyn in school.

2. The Rt. Rev. Christoph Keller, Jr., Tenth Bishop of the Episcopal Diocese of Arkansas (1970–1981), whose funeral homily will follow this one.

3. Daniel L. Migliore, *Faith Seeking Understanding: An Introduction to Christian Theology* (Grand Rapids, MI: William B. Eerdmans, 1991), 101.

4. For a concise presentation of Aquinas's thought on God and evil, and his doctrine of the *privatio boni*, I recommend Brian Davies, *The Thought of Thomas Aquinas* (Oxford: Clarendon / Oxford University Press, 1992), 89–97.

5. In a (rare) echo of Aquinas, Barth's German term for evil is *das Nichtige*, which translates "nothingness." As Barth emphasizes, this does not mean that evil is illusory, but that it is real in a "peculiar" fashion. "God takes it into account. He is concerned with it. He strives against it, resists and overcomes it." Karl Barth, *Church Dogmatics* III.3, ed. G.W. Bromiley and T.F. Torrance, trans. G. W. Bromiley and R. J. Ehrlich (Edinburgh: T & T Clark, 1960), 349–50.

6. Christoph Keller, III, "Sermon for the Twenty-Fourth Sunday after Pentecost" (Christ Episcopal Church, Hyde Park, MA, November 9, 1980).

7. 1 Cor. 15:19.

VI.

Christoph Keller, Jr.

Nice to Remember

December 22, 1915–May 19, 1995

Try to remember the kind of September
When life was slow and oh, so mellow.[1]

Driving south down the old road from Little Rock, I felt the past return. On my way out of town I had stopped at the store to see if they might have it and yes, they did, one copy: *The Fantasticks* "Original cast album, now available on cassette tape." The cassette was dusty, but it played. I was grateful. I would be five hours on the road. I wanted Dad's music for this ride, and *this* music more than any. It had been a feature album in his sermon repertoire. From the pew, we would watch him in the pulpit pause and look away to find the words, never in a hurry, just wait and let them come.

Try to remember when life was so tender
That love was an ember about to billow.

From all directions, we were making our way home to say goodbye. Mother, Caroline, Jim, and Robin had been there with him through the long ordeal.[2] Now, the rest of us rolled in—wave upon wave—five daughters and one son with spouses and progeny in tow. No one rang the doorbell. Robert Frost was also in his repertoire and we knew the line. "Home is the place where, when you have to go there, they have to take you in."[3]

We made it in time. Bedside, taking turns, we sat and

talked to him, prayed and wept for him. Tableside, we sipped or slurped good wine and gorged on the bayou soul food he adored. He would clean his plate of pork chops (fried), field peas, cornbread, and okra (fried). He would beg for seconds by evoking Oliver: "Please ma'am, I'd like some more."[4] He would hope for dessert: "Might there be a tiny scoop of low-fat sherbet?" At that, we would guffaw as he gave a wink and Mother rolled her eyes, because by "sherbet," everybody knew, he meant high-fat pie, pecan, "Honeycutt slice," with a scoop or three of ice cream.[5] It had been years since he could join us at the table. Now, at the end, we began to laugh again, and raise our glass to that good man we finally felt permission to remember.

> For now the winter is past,
> The rain is over and gone.[6]

He never quite knew what got him. Alzheimer's slips in on cat feet.[7] We wanted to help him understand, but the disease had stolen his understanding. The worst was in the middle stages, when he began to feel acute anxiety. He seemed tormented by some vestigial fear of being late.[8] He was needed somewhere. "Where are my car keys? Can you help me find them? I have to go right now!" We would try to assure him. "No Chris, no Dad, it's okay. Stay here with us." Nothing worked. He would pace back and forth and try the door, feeling trapped and helpless, sure that he in sleep his duty had forgot / while the devil slumbered not.[9] This disease is more terrible than advertised. My father suffered torments of the damned.

> Those who passed by derided him .... "He saved others; he cannot save himself .... He trusts in God; let God

deliver him. . . ." From noon on, darkness came over the whole land until three in the afternoon. And about three o'clock Jesus cried with a loud voice "Eli, Eli, lema sabachthani?" that is, "My God, my God, why have you forsaken me?"[10]

God as godforsaken—this was the paradox from which his faith was nourished. In Dad's era, bishops kept diaries. On the terrible day we learned that Robin's tumor was incurably malignant, in his he wrote: "The light shines in the darkness and the darkness has not overcome it."[11] That was John 1:5, the Revised Standard translation. The King James Version is curiously different: "The light shineth in darkness; and the darkness comprehended it not." Translators agree the darkness is at some kind of disadvantage to the light—but is this a lack of power or of comprehension? This is why they make us study Greek! The word is *katelaben,* which like our word *grasp* means both to understand (to grasp the truth) and to take control (to grasp the reins).[12] Darkness can neither wrap its mind, nor arms, around this light. This want is not reciprocal. On that hill outside Jerusalem, the light knows darkness inside out—and exploits it for the good. Christoph Keller, Jr. preached and lived these truths. For him, Christ crucified was light.

At home on his desk, dog-eared T.S. Eliot collections were companion to a thumb-worn Book of Common Prayer—sympatric treasuries of poetic contemplation. From the Prayer Book on Ash Wednesday: "Remember that you are dust, and to dust you shall return."[13] From Eliot's poem *Ash Wednesday*:

Lady, three white leopards sat under a juniper-tree
In the cool of the day, having fed to satiety

On my legs my heart my liver and that which had been
    contained
In the hollow round of my skull. And God said
Shall these bones live? shall these
Bones live? And that which had been contained
In the bones (which were already dry) said chirping:

....

We shine with brightness.[14]

As a pastor Dad spoke softly, while his presence mysteriously imparted strength. Love was the reason. "Love builds up," as St. Paul advised.[15] Faith and hope grow stronger. That quiet blend made Dad the priest and man he was. The night his father died, he gathered the children to tell us what had happened. I was seven years old and still remember how he broke it to us gently. "Children, I'm sad to tell you that your grandfather died today. I know you're sad too, but we don't need to worry about Papa. He's in good hands."

Psychologist friends have told me that, in dreams, a house can be a symbol for the soul. Suppose, for example, you dream one night of windows being added to your home. This could suggest an inward renovation taking place. From new sources, fresh air and good light are streaming in. So goes the theory. The symbolism fits with famous words in St. John's gospel. On his last night, Jesus gathers the disciples, who are panicked, to reassure them. "Let not your heart be troubled," he begins. For what comes next, I always choose King James: "In my Father's house are many mansions: if it were not so I would have told you. I go to prepare a place for you."[16] In pidgin theology, this translates: "In my Father's soul are many souls, mine soon to be included. When I die, this story isn't over. Not for me and not for you."

What kind of place does he prepare? Here is an answer

loved by Bishop Keller:

> Both a new world
> And the old made explicit, understood
> In the completion of its partial ecstasy,
> The resolution of its partial horror.[17]

That is Eliot, poetically defining the ineffable.

Dad had a favorite prayer for the departed. "Grant that, increasing in knowledge and love of you, he (or she) may go from strength to strength in the life of perfect service in your kingdom."[18] In proximity to death, he always found a time to pray that. He was steady through an era marked by doubt and rapid change. One Christmas, he asked himself "Where lies my faith?" Taking stock, he wrote: "I believe in Jesus Christ. He shows me important things and saves me in essential ways." How was he saved, and when? His answers blend eternity and time. "In a sense, once for all time I was saved at Calvary through love released. In another, I won't be safe until the last days when through the Resurrection hope there will be the discovery that death is not the end of life. In still another sense, I am in the life-long process of being saved. My Lord is available now, even in darkness. When I am in touch with Him, I believe that I am in touch with God."[19] In his diary, he wrote when Robin died: "From strength to strength he goes."[20] His next day's entry is from Eliot, ecstatic: "The communication of the dead is tongued with fire beyond the language of the living."[21]

Dad's faith was secure in the fact that he had known its truth in part already. Jesus promised this in his farewell. "Those who love me will keep my word, and my Father will love them, and we will come to them and make our home with them."[22] Chris Keller, Jr. knew it. He searched those words, took them to heart, and kept them. He treasured hymns that open doors and windows to the dove:

> Come down, O Love divine, seek thou this soul of mine, and visit it with thine own ardor glowing.[23]

His prayers were answered. The Spirit came. God was at home in him. Christ remained a gracious, honored presence in his life for eighty years. In this house the lights were on. They glowed warm through windows, attracting company. Richard Milwee, an Arkansas priest, said of Bishop Keller: "I loved being around him. I think everyone did. He made us feel better about ourselves and about life in general . . . . I was always happy when the bishop forgot, as he usually did, to take his crosier or his prayer book home with him after a parish visitation. Taking them back was just another opportunity to enjoy the pleasure of his company."[24]

The house has crumbled, as houses will. His savior moves on ahead to prepare the place for him. (Southerners and Holy Spirit practice reciprocating hospitality.) The Lord once known as guest and gracious ardor, in the heart of this most gracious man, is ready now as host to greet him, not as stranger, but as friend.

> Deep in December, it's nice to remember,
> Although you know the snow will follow.
> Deep in December, it's nice to remember,
> Without a hurt the heart is hollow.
> Deep in December, it's nice to remember,
> The fire of September that made us mellow.
> Deep in December, our hearts should remember
> And follow.[25]

Notes

1. "Try to Remember," *The Fantasticks,* music by Harvey Schmidt, lyrics by Tom Jones, opened Sullivan Street Playhouse, New York, NY, May 3, 1960.

2. My mother was Polly Keller. My parents raised five daughters and me. Caroline is the oldest sibling, Jim Theus is her husband, and Robin, whose father and namesake died when he was still an infant, is their youngest son. These four lived with my father on our Louisiana farm.

3. Robert Frost, "The Death of the Hired Man," *North of Boston* (New York: Henry Holt, 1917; A Public Domain Book), 8, Kindle.

4. Charles Dickens, *Oliver Twist* (London: Richard Bentley, 1838; Amazon Classics), 15, Kindle.

5. In Keller lingo, a "Keller slice" of pie or cake means health- and figure-friendly—i.e. puny. A "Honeycutt slice" means to hell with that. Julie Honeycutt Keller, my wife, spontaneously defined the terms, at this same dinner table, early in our marriage. Julie was served a see-through slice of caramel birthday cake she'd smelled baking in the kitchen through the afternoon. "That's a Keller slice," she said, returning the plate politely but emphatically. "I'd like a Honeycutt slice, which is about three—no, let's make it four—of that." The sentiment resonated and the phrasing stuck. Christoph Keller, Jr. was her kindred spirit.

6. Song of Sol. 2:11.

7. Carl Sandburg, "Fog," *Chicago Poems* (New York: Dover, 1994), loc. 415 of 968, Kindle.

8. From that concern, he had been never late for work, church, planes, or kickoffs.

9. "Come Labor On," The Hymnal 1982: According to the Use of the Episcopal Church (New York: Church Hymnal Corporation, 1982), Hymn 541.

10. Matt. 27:39–43, 45–46.

11. Christoph Keller, Jr., *A Bishop's Journal,* ed. Caroline Keller

54

Winter and Robert Johnson (Sedona, AZ: Memory Works Publishing, 2006), 266, entry for Jan. 1, 1980. This privately published volume was compiled from Bishop Keller's articles and diaries, first printed in *The Arkansas Churchman*, 1967–1980.

12. See entry for καταλαμβάνω in Frederick William Danker, ed., *A Greek-English Lexicon of the New Testament and Other Early Christian Literature*, 3rd ed, based on Walter Bauer's *Griechisch-deutsches Wörterbuch zu den Schriften des Neuen Testaments und der frühchristlichen Literatur*, sixth edition, ed. Kurt Aland et al. (Chicago: University of Chicago Press, 2000).

13. The Book of Common Prayer: According to the Use of the Episcopal Church (New York: Oxford University Press, 1990), 265.

14. T.S. Eliot, "Ash Wednesday," *Collected Poems 1909–1962* (New York: Harcourt, Brace & World, 1970), 87.

15. 1 Cor. 8:1.

16. John 14:1–2 (KJV).

17. Eliot, "Four Quartets," *Collected Poems,* 178.

18. "The Burial of the Dead: Rite One," Book of Common Prayer, 481, as adapted to modern English.

19. Christoph Keller, Jr., "Christmastide '71," *A Bishop's Journal*, 81–82.

20. *A Bishop's Journal*, 283, entry for Dec. 10, 1980.

21. *A Bishop's Journal*, 283, entry for Dec. 11–12, 1980, quoting Eliot, "Four Quartets," *Collected Poems*, 201.

22. John 14:23.

23. "Come Down O Love Divine," The Hymnal 1982, Hymn 516.

24. Richard Franklin Milwee, "Funeral Homily for the Rt. Rev. Christoph Keller, Jr., Tenth Bishop of Arkansas" (Trinity Episcopal Cathedral, Little Rock, AR, May 25, 1995). There were two services, and two sermons, for my father. I preached the funeral at St. James' Episcopal Church, Alexandria, Louisiana, on May 23, 1995. Richard was preacher for a memorial service in Little Rock two days later. For publication, I have slipped this line from Richard's sermon into mine.

25. "Try to Remember."

VII.

Caroline Murphy Keller

Winter

A Homily for Mother

January 5, 1922–September 21, 2014

About their first dance, she wrote:

That crisp late September evening I walked up the steps past Ham and Jam (who in college lore were supposed to bark every time a virgin passed by). . . . I remember exactly what I had on. . . . I had chosen a midnight blue velvet dress with a lace collar, princess style with a flared skirt that revealed just a bit of the knee. It had silver buttons down the front and I knew it was becoming. . . . I turned to meet the others, to find the blue eyes of a tall, brown-haired dead attractive young man looking intently at me. . . . My date was nice enough and a fair dancer, but we finally began switching partners, and I turned to find Chris looking at me with that intent gaze and quizzical smile, hand outstretched and saying in the most pleasant of voices, "Polly will you dance with me?" Indeed I would.[1]

"From There to Here," is the title of her memoir. She was a tough critic of her own work. It was frustrating, she would complain, not to be a better writer. As a reader, I wonder what was not to like, because I couldn't put it down. I suppose she measured herself by Eudora Welty.[2] Polly Keller Winter was a woman of exacting standards.[3]

A doting mother she was not, but she was attentive. Her parenting came with clear directions and feedback, which once arrived for me as a plate of spaghetti and green peas turned over on my head. At the dinner table she had some tolerance for back talk, but there were limits, as I learned. True to form, she left motherly instructions for her funeral, including the stipulation: "Homily by Chris. Homily, not eulogy," underlined. I should save the stories and wisecracks for the after-party. Already, I am on thin ice. You might be thinking: "Poor Polly, one full plate of green peas and spaghetti, topside, was not enough to make him mind."

Or maybe you are curious about "Homily, not eulogy," and wonder what's the difference. With Mother's help, I will speak to that. Along the way, I hope you won't mind that, as I read them, the rules for homilies at funerals leave room for laughs and reminiscing. I think they would have to. Karl Barth, a very serious theologian, described his craft as "the most beautiful of all the sciences." Music, laughter, and imagination are prerequisites. That means, I quote: "Sulky faces, morose thoughts and boring ways of speaking are intolerable."[4] From somewhere in the great beyond, my mother nods "Amen."

In so many ways, her life was charmed. She was born lucky in her parents, Charles and Bertie Murphy. She was lucky or smart in her selection of husbands—both Yankee gentlemen who attended Washington and Lee. Here is the finish to that story of her first dance with Dad.

> Yankee dancing was quite different from the El Dorado hop. . . . Never had I danced with anyone so smooth, so perfectly in time with the music, letting me get used to a simple two step, leading me lightly but firmly, then adding subtle variations, dips and pauses. *Ah* I thought, *This is dancing!* When the music ended, Chris said, "Polly, you are some dancer" and returned me to my uninspir-

ing date.[5]

The poor stiff. As I mentioned, Mother was a woman of exacting standards. Only Christoph Keller, Jr. and Clark B. Winter measured up.[6]

She was fortunate, knew it, and was grateful for it. But she had many children; and she lived for more than ninety years; and laws of probability, biology, and physics will have their say; and that all adds up to long and broad exposure to life's vicissitudes and heartbreaks. Trouble came early in adulthood. In the winter of 1940, Polly went into labor prematurely. She writes of losing that first baby.[7]

> The tiny baby girl was born the next morning and she never breathed.... I was stunned and devastated. I had never experienced any real grief or loss in my young life.... Chris, trying to comfort me, seemed able to put it in a perspective not available to me. Faced with the classic problem of pain and evil, my gut feeling was that God must be crazy.[8]

In this painful memory, Mother puts her finger on the difference between homily and eulogy. It's in this perceptive observation: "Chris seemed able to put it in a perspective not available to me." *Something* was clearly helping Dad— she saw that—but whatever this was, was opaque to her. It was not the words of Christian faith. She knew the words and they weren't helping. But some enigma in, above, and around those words had given her young husband a different footing in his grief. Its source is what a homily should try to bring to light.

As a priest, Dad used poetry to crack the nut. He died in 1995. Not long after, I opened a letter from Mother, just a brief note, clipped to a longer page in Dad's handwriting. She had found it going through his papers. It was part of a poem he had copied in his own hand and kept for a long time. The paper was old and cracked. Dad was naturally poetic, and for a time I guessed he might have written it himself. With some digging, I learned the author was the playwright and librettist Helen Kromer. Let's listen to these verses my father preserved, and my mother thought her son should see.

I open my mouth to speak
And the word is there,
Formed by the lips, the tongue,
The organ of voice. Formed by
The brain, transmitting the word
By breath.

I open my mouth to speak
And the word is there,
Traveling between us—caught
By the organ of hearing, the ear,
Transmitting the thought to the brain
Through the word.

Just so do we communicate—
You and I: the thought
From one mind leaping to another,
Given shape and form and substance,
So that we know and are known
Through the word.

But let me speak to my very small son
And the words mean nothing,

For he does not know my language.
And so I must show him: "This is your foot,"
I say; "and it is meant for walking."
I help him up: "Here is the way to walk!"
And one day "walking" shapes in his brain
With the word.

God had something to say to Man,
But the words meant nothing,
For we did not know his language.
And so we were shown: "Behold, the Man,"
He said. "This is the image, the thought
In my mind—Man as I mean him, loving and serving.
I have put Him in flesh. Now the Word
Has shape and form and substance
To travel between us. Let Him show forth love
Till one day 'loving' shapes in your brain
With the Word."[9]

"The Word" is the title of the poem.[10]

What sense do we make of life when it turns painful? Religion aside, we would have several ancient attitudes to choose from. I'll name three. One decision, as old as any, is that life just makes no sense at all. Macbeth gave voice to it, with cynical indifference, when he was told his wicked wife was dead. It must say a lot that we all know the speech and can quote the punch line: "Out, out, brief candle! Life's but a walking shadow. . . . It is a tale told by an idiot, full of sound and fury, signifying nothing."[11] Roughly opposite to that belief, and maybe just as old, is Hamlet's: "There's a divinity that shapes our ends, rough-hew them how we will."[12] Abraham Lincoln, early in his law career, liked to quote that to his partner William Herndon.[13] Was that faith? Later it would be, almost, but it wasn't yet for Lincoln. At that stage in life, he saw (and feared) the shaping forces as uncaring and impersonal. "The fates settled things," he thought, and like Polly in her grief he felt those gods were crazy.[14] The stoic Epictetus offered the ancient world a third, more attractive point of view. From him, students learned to humbly recognize the smallness of our place within the grand scheme; to appreciate life's pleasures; and to bravely and dispassionately (i.e. "stoically") accept the inevitable vicissitudes. Walker Percy, who well knew the genteel southern world that he and Mother were both raised to inhabit, regarded stoicism as its native outlook. Along with its terrible taint, that old south had a greatness to it, Percy wrote, that "had always a stronger Greek flavor than it ever had a Christian."[15] Cynicism, fatalism, stoicism: those three are perennial philosophies. The first abandons hope; down the second road lies madness; for high-minded southerners, the third has been an attractive option. Polly suffered early from lost children; later she endured her faithful, blue-eyed husband's slow descent into dementia; and, by the age of ninety-two, she had lost many dear ones. She never lost hope; she did not go mad; and, genteel and brave she was—but never stoic.

A Christian homily is the offer of an outlook in which a partial truth, or guess at truth, from each of these old secular philosophies is drawn into the sacred meaning of the Word. Thomas Aquinas, for the first example, sometimes sounds like Epictetus.[16] Read the *Summa Theologiae*, and find human self-centeredness dissolved in stoic fashion. Our world was not set up for short-term human safety or convenience. God has a universe to care for, not just Jack and Jill, who should mind their feet when they set out for water.[17] But this universe was made with purposes in mind that would surprise a stoic. Walker Percy, of that old south stock, read the *Summa* while in quarantine for tuberculosis.

He was converted to Christian faith, drawn by the beauty of the Word.

Lincoln also had a finger on a truth about the world and God. Faith agrees with fatalism that even the strongest of us do not control events or circumstances. Something in and beyond the world and life moves towards us, shaping outcomes. Faith identifies this moving force as God. Lincoln, who grew with time into a question-asking, embryonic faith, dropped the talk of fates and began to speak of providence that settles things like slavery and civil war.[18] Even when concealed, which it almost always is, providence moves with, and long ahead of us. In the Word, faith sees the secret brought to light that God, and I quote Barth because he says it beautifully, "is never absent, passive, non-responsible or impotent, but always present, active, responsible, and omnipotent. He is never dead, but always living; never sleeping, but always awake; never uninterested, but always concerned . . . [and] even where he seems to wait, . . . always holding the initiative."[19]

Now the plot thickens. Macbeth was not all wrong. Christian faith requires two eyes, by which I mean it views one truth with depth from two perspectives. Christ is the prime example. We regard him both as human and divine—"truly man" and "truly God"—according to the Council of Chalcedon.[20] That gives his ministry, at every step, two meanings, as both a human action and an act of God. Theologians sometimes speak of this as "double agency." I know this because I am a theologian, and I wrote a dissertation titled "Darwin's Science in Chalcedonian Imagination: Barth, Double Agency, and Theistic Evolution."[21] It is a tome. Guess who read it. That's right, my mother. Polly read, marked, and understood her son's giant homework paper stem to stern. She approved of it too, she told me. If you asked her if you should read it, she answered "just the introduction and conclusion." I will spare you even that, to save your reading time for *Macbeth* or *Harry Potter*. "Darwin's Science in Chalcedonian Imagination" shows why Christian tradition could faithfully absorb Charles Darwin's scientific revolution. Conceptually, they fit through scripture's familiarity with double agency. God's creative work is not in competition with the world's, any more than Harry Potter's magic in the books competes with J. K. Rowling's magic in creating them. This is why Macbeth, the guilty cynic, had a point—the same point made in scripture by the righteous Job. The universe is not enchanted. Laws of chemistry, biology, and physics, with those of sociology, psychology, and economics, proceed according to their own devices and design, generating motion, money, music, sound, and fury—often signifying nothing special. So yes, Barth writes, God is awake, concerned, and active, but the desert is still dreary and the night still dark.[22]

In this union of God's doing and the world's, our lives mysteriously unfold.[23] Our God-given freedom spices up the mystery. It is a spacious union, making ample room for ups and downs through dreary days and bright ones. Ecclesiastes maps the oscillations in another speech that everybody knows and sees the truth of. There is "a time to weep, and a time to laugh; a time to mourn, and a time to dance."[24] Barth names other pairs that God made room and time for: "prosperity and adversity," "peril and protection," and "victory and defeat." God is Lord through all of it, he says—and this is a man who lived through two world wars—but God has different ways of being Lord.[25] In Christ, God reigns in one way from the cross and in quite another from the empty tomb. That gospel truth keeps Christian faith alert for God through bitter times and sweet. While daily at risk, we are eternally secure. We are "afflicted . . . but not crushed," "struck down but not destroyed," and "perplexed, but not driven to despair."[26] That was St. Paul's review of life in the Chalcedonian regime. In it, Polly Keller found her footing.

Mom, I hope that was homily enough to suit you.

"The postman rings twice," they say. He did for Polly. When Jim Theus said last rites for Mother Saturday, it was her second time to hear them in the past twelve months. Last winter, she had badly cracked her hip, and surgery was recommended. At her age, that was risky. At her age, she didn't care. "Where do I sign?" she said. On the operating table, her vital signs went south. "Call the family," said the doctor, and they sent her home to die. The word went out and we came in. At Inglewood, we gathered bedside.[27] From the Prayer Book, I led the Litany at Time of Death—but holding back the final prayer. Mother seemed to be unconscious, drawing shallow breaths in fits and starts. "Mother," I said loudly, "I am saving the last prayer until I know for sure you need it." If she could hear that, she would know the prayer I meant—the one that begins "Depart . . . ." Thinking that time could come at any moment, we waited for the end. Meanwhile, down the road at Hard Times, her grandson Sam Bonsey was entertaining guests, Harvard classmates who'd come south for a sample of the redneck highlife: shooting cans, dodging snakes, and hunting hogs.[28] The trip had been planned for months, and of course Sam's "Mamá" was all for it. Cancelling was pointless, so they carried on. Taking turns, we sat with Mother through the night. Come morning, she was still here—and beginning to perk up a bit, it seemed. Gradually, her breaths got steadier and stronger. Vital signs improved. Then, she slowly cracked an eyelid. There we were, her five remaining children standing by her bed, and she knew why. She absorbed the moment. "Well," she asked, "Did Sam get a pig?"

He did.

Our funny mother lived—to love and make us laugh an-

other year. More than once, she danced. And now it is time
for me to finish what I started:

Depart O Christian Soul.
In the Name of God the Father Almighty who created
you;
In the Name of Jesus Christ who redeemed you.
In the Name of the Holy Spirit who sanctifies you.
May your rest be this day in peace,
And your dwelling place in the Paradise of God.[29]

Notes

1. Caroline Murphy Keller Winter, "Polly," *From There to Here: A Life* (Sedona, AZ: The Memory Works, 2010), 97–98. Printed by author.

2. From 1961 to 1967 our family lived in Jackson, Mississippi, where Dad served as Dean of St. Andrew's Cathedral. Miss Charlotte Capers, from St. Andrew's, was a frequent dinner guest, legendary raconteur, and favorite family friend. Charlotte happened also to be the best friend (BFF) of Jackson native Eudora Welty. Through Charlotte, Mother came to know Eudora. She admired her greatly as a person and, of course, a writer.

3. About her nickname. Mother was born in El Dorado, Arkansas, at an exuberant, chaotic moment in that town's history—the discovery of oil under and around the city limits. Her mother of three, Bertie, and oil prospecting father, Charles, couldn't find a moment quiet enough to mutually decide what to name their newborn. Since she was an easy baby, "a Pollyanna," they called her Polly for the meantime. When they finally named her Caroline Patience Murphy for the record, it was too late. To everyone, she was already and forever Polly.

4. Karl Barth, *Church Dogmatics* II.1, ed. G. W. Bromiley and T. F. Torrance, trans. T. H. L. Parker, et al. (Edinburgh: T & T Clark, 1957), 656. Later in this section (page 666), Barth writes that God has provided that he should be attractive to human beings, and worthy of our love, and "has done this simply by giving them joy, and given them joy by being beautiful."

5. Winter, *From There to Here*, 98.

6. Chris and Polly met when she attended Mary Baldwin College, up the Shenandoah from Washington and Lee. In the years after college, they remained active in Washington and Lee alumni programs. Near the end of Dad's life, Mother met Clark Burritt Winter, who had recently lost his wife of many years, while attending one such program. After Dad's death, Clark called Polly, leading to ten very happy years of mar-

68

riage, until Clark's death in 2006.

7. She would lose two more, both girls.

8. Winter, *From There to Here*, 138.

9. "The Word," *For Heaven's Sake: A Musical Review in Two Acts*, music by Frederick Silver, book and lyrics by Helen Kromer (Boston: Baker's Plays, 1961), 18, https://books.google.com/books?id=3xp-c0JGO-7gC&printsec=frontcover&source=gbs⊠ge⊠summary⊠r&-cad=0#v=onepage&q&f=false.

10. Dad left a filing note on his transcription of the poem. It was one word: "Incarnation." God the Son "became incarnate from the Virgin Mary," according to the creed. This was Christoph Keller, Jr.'s favorite doctrine. It maps God's journey earthward, into human history, to give us eyes and feet, kindling imagination. This is a two-way trek, "from there to here" and back again. God descends, with us to live and die. On his ascent, we rise.

11. *Macbeth* Act V, Scene v, lines 23–28, *The Riverside Shakespeare,* ed. G. Blakemore Evans et al. (Boston: Houghton Mifflin, 1974), 1337.

12. *Hamlet* Act V, Scene ii, lines 10–11, *Riverside Shakespeare*, 1181.

13. David Herbert Donald, *Lincoln* (New York: Simon & Schuster, 1995), 15.

14. Allen C. Guelzo, *Abraham Lincoln: Redeemer President* (Grand Rapids, MI: William B. Eerdmans, 1999), loc. 1605 of 7046, Kindle.

15. Walker Percy, "Stoicism in the South," *Signposts in a Strange Land* (New York: Farrar, Straus & Giroux, 1991), 84.

16. For Epictetus as an important influence on early (and later) Christian reflection, see Diogenes Allen, *Philosophy for Understanding Theology* (Atlanta: John Knox Press, 1985), 65–69.

17. See Thomas Aquinas, *Summa Theologiae*, part one, question 22, "The Providence of God," article 2, the reply to the second objection.

18. "I claim not to have controlled events, but confess plainly that events have controlled me." "Now at the end of three years struggle the nation's condition is not what either party, or any man devised, or expected. God alone can claim it." Donald, *Lincoln*, 514. Lincoln's reflections on God's purposeful direction of the war shine through his *sui*

generis Second Inaugural Address.

19. Barth, CD III.3, 13.

20. "Definition of the Union of the Divine and Human Natures in the Person of Christ," *The Council of Chalcedon, 451 A.D.*, Book of Common Prayer, 864.

21. Christoph Keller, III, "Darwin's Science in Chalcedonian Imagination: Barth, Double Agency and Theistic Evolution" (ThD diss., General Theological Seminary, 2009). The title alludes to George Hunsinger, who wrote that Barth's was a "deeply imbued Chalcedonian imagination." George Hunsinger, *How to Read Karl Barth: The Shape of His Theology* (New York: Oxford University Press, 1991), 85.

22. Barth, CD III.3, 189.

23. Barth describes this as "a difficult union of opposites." CD III.3, 97.

24. Eccles. 3:4.

25. Barth, CD III.3, 19.

26. 2 Cor. 4:8–10.

27. Inglewood is the family farm outside Alexandria, Louisiana. It was in its then-decrepit antebellum house, before electricity, that Polly and Chris had spent their wedding night in 1940, and it was there that each of them would breathe their last.

28. Hard Times was the name of what had once been the adjoining farm. My sister Caroline raised her family there. Polly's grandson Sam Bonsey, a New Englander, has long loved the Louisiana farm and visits often.

29. "Ministration at the Time of Death," Book of Common Prayer, 464.

VIII.

Naomi Elizabeth Gray May

Multiply by Two

July 2, 1929–February 21, 2018

Naomi Elizabeth Gray, "Nonny," was born July 2, 1929 in Memphis—a proud city. In *The Reivers*, Faulkner has Lucius Priest say of Memphis: "Where else could anyone in north Mississippi want to go?"[1] That feeling was pervasive in the Delta, east Arkansas included. You probably have heard what David Cohn said, that the Delta "begins in the lobby of the Peabody Hotel [in Memphis] and ends on Catfish Row in Vicksburg."[2] That was true going south. What it doesn't say is something we know here in Little Rock: that the Delta's western endpoint is Scott, Arkansas. In 1982, when Nonny moved out from Little Rock to Scott—a fifteen-minute drive straight east—she was going home.

The stock market crashed when Nonny was just shy of five months old, but she was protected through the Great Depression by her father's well-earned prosperity as the first and best radiologist in Memphis. She was twelve when Japan attacked Pearl Harbor. Imagine that as a formative experience. Her high school memories of St. Mary's Episcopal were punctuated by war news: Midway, D-Day, and such. VJ-Day came a week or so before she started senior year.

One day Nonny's daughter Rachel, who had been raised with a younger generation's sensibility, was slightly shocked to discover a pistol in her mother's handbag. Growing up, I had a similar experience. One night we had a burglar in our house, downstairs. We had called the cops and I was perched at the top of the stairs, more or less to guard the family. From behind, my mother tapped me on the shoulder and handed me her shotgun, loaded. "You might need this," she said, not scared. For southern women of that generation, surrendering to force was not Plan A.

Gardening was Nonny's genius. That knack runs strong in women of the family. Nonny and her sisters acquired it from their mother and passed it down to their own daughters, along with digging forks and pruning sheers. Last Monday night, Rachel was up late with thoughts of her mother, feeling her loss. She reflected on Nonny's love for growing things and stubborn faith in their potential:

> My mother never ever accepted that anything was dead. She could bring anything back. Often these plants would be too scraggly to sell. But she would put them somewhere in the greenhouse, and she was patient. And hardly ever did anything really die. I never had the patience for that, and I have always thrown out the plants that seemed beyond redemption . . . until recently. This morning I was watering, and I have a little corner where I kept a few plants that were neglected when I was out of town, and they were pretty far gone. But this little corner is so pretty now. Everything looks lovely. I was not really conscious of this switch I made to nurture these plants back. But I know my mom always did that, and I think I wanted to take that from her.

I will call that a Christian education.

Nonny also grew children: two girls and two boys. In *The Fantasticks*, the old off-Broadway musical, two dads compare childrearing to plant-rearing—unfavorably:

> Plant a radish.
> Get a radish.

Never any doubt.
That's why I love vegetables;
You know what you're about!

Plant a turnip.
Get a turnip.
Maybe you'll get two.
That's why I love vegetables;
You know that they'll come through!

They're dependable!
They're befriendable!
They're the best pal a parent's ever known!
While with children,
It's bewilderin'.
You don't know until the seed is nearly grown
Just what you've sown.[3]

With so many baby-boomers underfoot, it's no mystery that our parents loved that show and kept it running more than forty years. They thought they'd planted Frank Sinatra but reaped the Grateful Dead.

In the annals of slightly shocking revelations, one of the doozies is Mr. Darwin's discovery that those radishes and turnips are we humans' distant kin.[4] So are tigers. This family secret came to light in 1858.[5] But our shared attributes with animals and plants had long before been recognized by Thomas Aquinas, the theologian. This comes to the front in Aquinas's description of the human soul.[6] People now tend to think of souls as invisible and simple, if they believe in them at all. Aquinas saw them hiding in plain sight. Souls are not something that we have; they are what we are. And, far from simple, what we are is complex and multilayered, with radish-like and tiger-like dimensions. With vegetables, we share capacities for nourishment, defense, and reproduction. Along with other animals, we feel passion. Aquinas named eleven emotions: love, desire, delight, hate, aversion, sorrow, fear, daring, hope, despair, and anger.[7] Those are the colors of our feelings. They please, entertain, and torment us. Some of these feelings do our tiger cousins likewise. We notice this and truly sympathize.

Children are bewilderin' because they're made of more than radish-like and tiger-like material. They are also born with seeds of *God*-like powers. They will know that two and two make four. Reason, we call that, and it also sorts out true from false and bad from good. Moreover, children can decide either "I will" or "I won't" and behave accordingly. "Freedom" we call this power to choose between alternatives, and it is neither passion's master nor its slave. Radishes cannot make commitments. People can, and we can break them, and there is often damage when we do.

Nonny was a writer with talent. As Julliard is to music, so is the Iowa Writers' Workshop to poetry and fiction. Flannery O'Connor and John Irving, for example, are alumni. Marilynne Robinson, my favorite living writer, taught there. She won the Pulitzer Prize for fiction for her novel *Gilead*. That is where Nonny went to college.

Gilead is the story of an old man with a young son. The man is John Ames, retired pastor of a Midwestern small town congregation. Ames suffers from a heart defect and knows his days are numbered. His little boy will grow up without him. One morning, Ames watches over as the boy, still in pajamas, plays on the floor with a coloring book and crayons. When a crayon breaks, he tries to put it back together, unsuccessfully. After every attempted fix had failed, son looks up to father with a penetrating glance that seems to question: So this is life? "Sometimes it has seemed to me,"

Ames muses, "that you were looking back through life, back through troubles I pray you'll never have, asking me to kindly explain myself."[8] So it is by way of explanation that, with such time as may remain, Ames pens a (book-length) message-in-a-bottle for his child to have and read when grown.

When the grown son meets his father in these pages, he will read how Ames was smitten by a woman decades younger: Lila, the boy's mother. Ames describes feeling foolish for his feelings—he was hopelessly too old and had Lila not taken the initiative, she might never have known he loved her. When she did take it, Ames was more than slightly shocked. "At that point I began to suspect, as I have from time to time, that grace has a grand laughter in it."[9] There it is again: a Christian education.

Here is more of it from Ames: "Love is holy," he writes, "because it is like grace—the worthiness of its object is never really what matters."[10] Let's take it slow. Listen.

Love is holy.

The love Nonny's sons and daughters have for their mother is holy.

It is holy because it is like grace.

It is like grace, in that her worthiness is "never really what matters" to their love.

As for love, we know this without being told. Nonny's children know they love their mother and that in this love, her worthiness is incidental. They longed for her at times when she was absent, and love was in the longing. They cared for her when she was helpless, and love was in the caring. They grieve her now, and love is in the grieving. At times, their love was in forgiving. In none of this is there a judgment, yes or no, on her deserving it. It is just how they felt and what they did.

We know love as naturally as we know rain and music. Right now, we see, hear, and feel it in this room. About love, the truth we may have missed is: it is holy, and it is holy for its family resemblance to grace. As for grace, people wonder what it means and are shy to ask. If that is you, turn Ames's analogy around: grace is like love—the worthiness of its recipient is never really what matters. The love Ames and Lila feel for their little boy, and Nonny's children's longing for their departed mother, are images of grace. Ames informs his son he doesn't have to earn his parents' love. He has it by existing. "You see how it is godlike to love the *being* of someone. You*r* *existence* is a delight to us."[11] So grace is God's delight, like ours, in Nonny May: this woman whose children describe her as "a blend of Hunter S. Thompson and Eudora Welty"—a pistol-packing literary Delta Lady! What's not to love?! Your laughter is Christian education. It doesn't say that what we do with life is unimportant. It says that grace and love will happen anyway.

Let's think about heaven.

Ames's best friend is another old minister named Robert Boughton. Occasionally, the two men talk of heaven. Being well-schooled Calvinists, they know better than to try to say too much. For his son, Ames writes: "We know nothing about heaven, or very little, and I think Calvin is right to discourage curious speculations on things the Lord has not seen fit to reveal to us."[12] When God holds information back, there are reasons. Still, Ames does venture an opinion on a question we all have. When we think of our parents on the other shore, should we imagine them as old? And what about a baby sister whose life was cut short? When you meet her, is she grown? That makes sense to Ames, who says to his son, "I believe the soul in Paradise must enjoy something nearer to a perpetual vigorous adulthood than to any other state we know. At least that is my hope."[13] In *Field of Dreams*, Kevin Costner meets his long-dead father, in Iowa, for a heavenly game of catch.[14] The older man is younger than his son by ten or fifteen years. I love that hope a lot. Boughton says something I may love even more. I am quoting Ames, warming to our subject. "Boughton says he has more ideas about heaven every day. He said, 'Mainly, I just think about the splendors of the world and multiply by two. I'd multiply by ten or twelve if I had the energy. But two is more than sufficient for my purposes.' So he's just sitting there multiplying the feel of the wind by two, multiplying the smell of the grass by two."[15] Out in Scott, looking to the fields at night, Nonny might multiply a harvest moon.

And why not? The gist of these ideas is that life on earth resembles life beyond, while paling by comparison. They are not flights of fancy. Their source is scripture, where they are known to be important. We see them in Paul's tent–house and moon–sun comparisons: "For we know that if the earthly tent we live in is destroyed, we have a building from God, a house not made with hands, eternal in the heavens."[16] Paul knows tents, so that's what he would multiply. For those who don't know tents, he multiplies the moon. "There is one glory of the sun, and another glory of the moon."[17] What multiple of moonlight is the sun's? That is Paul's measure of the change from earthly life to paradise. We know light when we see it. When we see God it will be déjà vu, to the power of ten or twelve.

Do you know who else appreciated plants? Someone who said "I am the vine, you are the branches;"[18] and this: "Unless a grain of wheat falls into the earth and dies, it remains just a single grain; but if it dies, it bears much fruit."[19] *A grain of wheat who falls into the earth and dies.* That is a self-portrait of the Son of God. *Fruitful branches.* That was he describing us, potentially, who may think of ourselves as too far gone. *She could bring anything back.* That is a daughter's praise for Naomi May, who *never ever accepted that anything was dead.* She was a parable. And now she rests.

Notes

1. William Faulkner, *The Reivers* (New York: Vintage International, 1992), 57, eBook.

2. David L. Cohn, *God Shakes Creation* (New York: Harper & Brothers, 1935), 17, quoted in Justin Faircloth, "William Faulkner's Memphis: Architectural Identity, Urban Edge Condition, and Prostitution in 1905 Memphis," *Inquiry: The University of Arkansas Undergraduate Research Journal* 6, no. 1 (2005), 1, https://scholarworks.uark.edu/inquiry/vol6/iss1/4.

3. "Plant a Radish," *The Fantasticks*.

4. Charles Darwin, *The Origin of Species: By Means of Natural Selection, Or the Preservation of Favored Races in the Struggle for Life*, 1993 Modern Library Edition (New York: Modern Library, 1993). As he opens the concluding chapter, Darwin offers "descent with modification through variation and natural selection" as a perfectly succinct description of the evolutionary process as he understands it. The implied common ancestry of all species, including *Raphanus sativus*, *Panthera tigris*, and *Homo sapiens*, will become more conspicuously the theme of Darwin's second big book, *The Descent of Man*.

5. Alfred Russel Wallace was also deservedly given credit for the discovery, which was first presented on July 1, 1858 to the Linnean Society of London. This was a low-key affair: a third-party reading of a paper jointly authored by Darwin and Wallace. For that important story of some events that put Darwin's scholarly integrity to a severe test, one that he passed with flying colors, see E. Janet Browne, *Charles Darwin: The Power of Place* (Princeton, NJ: Princeton University Press, 2002), 14–42. Darwin's *Origin of Species* was published to great fanfare the following year.

6. For a brilliant book on the subject of souls, see Nancey Murphy, *Bodies and Souls, or Spirited Bodies?* (Cambridge: Cambridge University Press, 2006). Murphy's overview of Aquinas's "elaborate account of

the hierarchically ordered faculties or powers of the soul," which I follow here, is found on pages 14 and 15, Kindle.

7. Murphy, *Bodies and Souls*, 15.

8. Marilynne Robinson, *Gilead* (New York: Picador, 2004), 9, Kindle.

9. Robinson, *Gilead*, 235.

10. Robinson, 238.

11. Robinson, 155.

12. Robinson, 188–89.

13. Robinson, 189.

14. *Field of Dreams*, directed by Phil Alden Robinson (1989; Universal Pictures).

15. Robinson, 167.

16. 2 Cor. 5:1

17. 1 Cor. 15:41.

18. John 15:5.

19. John 12:24.

IX.

John Fredrick Forster, Jr.
Northbound Train

December 18, 1942–May 7, 2019

I wish I was a headlight, on a northbound train.
I'd shine my light through the cool Colorado rain.

Those lines are from "I Know You Rider," a song so old no one knows who wrote it. The Grateful Dead began to play it early in their history, and performed it live several hundred times. I mention this because the Honorable John Fredrick Forster, Jr., United States Magistrate Judge for the Eastern District of Arkansas, according to my sources, was a Deadhead. That must be an exaggeration, because a full immersion Deadhead commitment was incompatible with holding down a steady job, much less a career as judge and law professor. Let's just say Judge Forster loved the Grateful Dead. I did too, and in my opinion, they were at their best between Woodstock (1969) and Watergate (1974), and at their peak in the summer of 1972, which was when, on tour in Europe, they recorded "I Know You Rider."[1]

I know you rider, gonna miss me when I'm gone.
Gonna miss your baby, from rolling in your arms.

John's working life, but more than that his view of life, was grounded in the law. Law is more than a career choice. Richard Hooker defined law as any sort of rule "whereby actions are framed."[2] You probably haven't heard of Richard Hooker, and may be wondering what firm he was with and what was his area of practice. I hope you won't hold it against him that Hooker was not an Arkansas lawyer, but an English theologian, a very influential one, back in the day of Queen Elizabeth I. That influence trickles down to us. John Locke, in his two *Treatises of Government*, draws support from "the judicious Hooker," as Locke likes to call him, in building Locke's case for freedom and equality as birthrights. This is Locke, for example, in the *Second Treatise*: "This *equality* of men by nature, the judicious Hooker looks upon as so evident in itself, and beyond all question, that he makes it the foundation of that obligation to mutual love amongst men, on which he builds the duties they owe one another." [3] Do you see? Hooker's premise blazed the trail for Thomas Jefferson: this truth that all people are created equal is "self-evident." Philosophically, this was a revolution. The established view had been that we are born subservient to kings. Against that old, entrenched idea, Locke's new philosophy prevailed. Our founders built this nation on it.

So laws are rules that govern actions. This applies from God above on down to city council. People have been busy making laws since cave dwellers learned that the rule of every man for himself was not a recipe for happiness. "Positive law" is the philosopher's term for these human-made rules that frame our life in common. Positive laws are the stuff Judge Forster had to do with daily. What's on the books? he'd ask; and, How does that apply to the case at hand? The judicious Forster wore his robe as though it were the mantle of a sacred duty, and it was.

Hooker was among the first philosophers to apply the word "law" to natural sciences.[4] Laws of physics frame the movements of the stars and planets; laws of chemistry govern springtime shifts in water molecules from cloud to snow to ice-cold falling rain.

I wish I was a headlight, on a northbound train.
I'd shine my light through the cool Colorado rain.

So much is lawful on that train! Suppose we are waiting for it at a mountaintop depot. First, we notice the headlight winding upward from the valley, because, by a rule of some sort, light moves at 186,000 miles per second. Some time goes by. Then we pick up the chug and churn of rolling steel, on sound waves moving slowly, relative to light, at 767 miles per hour. Finally, the train itself rolls in, its crawl up mountain curves constrained, by laws of gravity and friction, to forty miles per hour through the rainy night. That is still good time to us. John was a runner, fit and trim, much faster than your average judge or Deadhead. In the mountains, he might cover thirty, even forty, miles per day. With laws of nature, there's no fighting City Hall.

Here is a conundrum for a law professor/judge. What do we do when a law of one kind encroaches on a different kind of law's domain? In Locke's *Second Treatise*, he recognizes natural moral laws, discernible to reason, that *do* fight City Hall from time to time. For example, Locke identifies a natural right to self-defense.[5] Any human legislation that would contradict that right is overruled by this moral law of nature. Judge Forster, what say you to that?

Here is another. In church, we promulgate God's law. We vow not to steal or murder, among other things, and to love our neighbors as ourselves. What are we to do when caught in a conflict between a law of God—in President Lincoln's immortal phrase, "the right as God gives us to see the right"[6]—and a law of city, state, or country? Judge Forster admired Dr. Martin Luther King, Jr.—so much so that this funeral service opened with Ian David Coleman's *The Trumpet Sounds Within-A-My Soul*, a musical paean to King's also-immortal "I Have a Dream" speech from the steps of the Lincoln Memorial. In the south, King challenged manmade laws enforcing racial segregation. When persuasion failed, King sometimes disobeyed the laws. "An unjust law is no law at all" he would explain, quoting Augustine. When asked what makes a law unjust, King would answer with Aquinas: "An unjust law is a human law that is not rooted in eternal law and natural law."[7] "God walks with us," King declared. "He has placed within the very structure of the universe certain absolute moral laws. . . . If we disobey them, they will break us."[8] (The converse, also true, is even more important: when human laws or nature's laws have broken us, the eternal law of God will save us. Hold that thought, I'm coming back to it.) But John was sworn to uphold his nation's law as written. When written laws conflict with moral laws, natural or divine, that spells trouble, if not crisis, for a faithful thinker like John—something to ponder in his chambers, or on early morning runs.

This is a guess, but I believe his duty would have been clear to John. By oath, he was conscience-bound to apply the laws of state even when he saw a higher law above them. We have different parts to play in American society. Preachers, professors, and reformers have more latitude than cops and judges, who cannot enforce the law and also break it. King had his duties, and John his, and each should play his own part conscientiously, for the common good. That way we render unto Caesar and to God.

Or maybe I've guessed wrong, and John would disagree. If so, I would have loved chewing the conundrum with him, an old philosophical bone, with our music on, low volume, as soundtrack. Eventually one of us would have enough of talking, reach over to the amp, and crank up the music full blast.

Lay down last night, Lord I could not take my rest.
Lay down last night, Lord I could not take my rest.
My mind was wandering like the wild geese in the west.

"When human laws or nature's laws have broken us, the eternal law of God will save us." I mentioned Thomas Aquinas, whom I've grown more to appreciate in recent years.[9] For the longest, his formality was Greek to me. A book that helped was Timothy McDermott's "concise translation" of Aquinas's giant *Summa Theologiae*. ("Concise" works out to six hundred pages on the dot.) McDermott hides the sausage-making logic and serves up the fully cooked conclusions. His seventh chapter is my favorite: "Human Life as a Journey to God." It means that Jerry Garcia had his wish.[10] We are a northbound train.

Are you ready for a truth that makes us free? Our journey's end is blissful. To Aquinas, perfect means complete. John lay down to take his rest in perfect happiness in God. This heavenly promise is as stout as the command to love our neighbor.

In the meantime, our happiness is, formally speaking, less than perfect. That is another piece of truth that I find helpful. Think of it as we might a State Department health and safety bulletin for travelers in certain foreign lands. "Happiness: what to expect in southern climates." Here's my concise translation. Number 1: Earthly happiness wanders like those wild geese in the west. It splashes in and rests a while; then up and flies; then circles back; and so on. Number 2: That this happiness is restless doesn't mean that it is in short supply. It joins us rolling in our baby's arms, ecstatic. It finds us in a bathrobe, sitting in a front porch rocker, serenely sipping morning coffee, savoring a gentle Colorado rain. Such moments are as plentiful as water. Seldom does a day pass without at least a sip of one, even if only as a happy memory of better days gone by, or an ecstatic dream, like Dr. King's, of brighter ones to come.

Aquinas puts his finger on our problem: "We can be partially happy in this life but not completely and truly."[11] How so? He provides a few examples, some of which surprise us. When we use the word "unhappy," we are typically describing an emotion. "Sad" and "miserable" are synonyms. Aquinas draws a wider circle. For instance, he writes that there are ills in life that cannot be avoided, and we nod. Then he names one, "ignorance," and we say, "What?" We'd been told "ignorance is bliss." To Aquinas, it is tragic. Another example: "unbalanced attachments." That means we need or want too much of this, and not enough of that. Again, we're puzzled. What's unhappy about needs or wants, if we can supply them? Aquinas is thinking about our journey north. Too-powerful attachments throw our compass out of whack; too-tepid ones can too.[12] But Aquinas isn't always esoteric. "Bodily pains" are on his list. Even little children nod at that: by age ten, or five, or one, they know. Then he touches us old folk where we hurt all over. We desire the good things we have to last, he writes, but "in this life they pass away."[13] He sure did get that right. We miss our babies when they're gone.

About death, Aquinas states the facts. "Life itself passes away, though by nature we desire it and wish it to last and shrink from death."[14] It's one of my favorite things he says on any topic. Faith gives nature its due. "I will survive" is nature's law, an animal rule that frames human actions toward survival—with divine approval. Nature is afraid of death, an unhappy fear that has served our species well enough through evolution. Faith is not afraid of death but takes nature's side in hating it. "The last enemy to be destroyed is death," said Paul.[15] Faith knows life on earth as gift, and the loss of it as grievous. For John's large family, and hundreds of friends, separation is the heartache of the present hour.

Let's hear it again: "The last enemy to be destroyed is death." Think of the pain and grief of John's life blissfully dissolved. Why would we think that? Because love is God's eternal law. How can we say this? Because we see it in the Bible, when the death of Jesus, lawfully ordained by Pontius Pilate, is overruled by superior authority. Roman law was broken on creation's constitution. In church, that's what we celebrate at Easter; and on Sundays, which are echoes of it; and at funerals, which are too. It's our light through mountain darkness and the cool Colorado rain.

Notes

1. The Grateful Dead, "I Know You Rider," *Europe '72*, Warner Brothers Records 3WX 2668, 1972. All the blocked verses in this sermon are from this song.

2. Richard Hooker, *Of the Laws of Ecclesiastical Polity: Preface, Book I, Book VIII*, ed. Arthur Stephen McGrade, Cambridge Texts in the History of Political Thought (New York: Cambridge University Press, 1989), xx.

3. John Locke, *Second Treatise of Government*, ed. C.B. Macpherson (Cambridge: Hackett, 1980), 8, Kindle.

4. This is according to Arthur Stephen McGrade, who writes: "Hooker is one of the first writers to use the term 'law of nature' in the modern sense of a physical law, in contrast with the Stoic and medieval sense (which he also employs) of universally valid moral principles." Hooker, *Laws*, xxii.

5. Locke, *Second Treatise*, 14–15.

6. Abraham Lincoln, Second Inaugural Address, *The Annals of America*, vol. 9, 1858–1865 (Chicago: Encyclopaedia Britannica, 1976), 556.

7. Martin Luther King, Jr., Letter from Birmingham Jail, April 16, 1963, *Why We Can't Wait* (Boston: Beacon Press), 92, Kindle.

8. Martin Luther King, Jr., *Strength to Love* (Boston: Beacon Press, 1981), 115, Kindle.

9. The turning point was a midcareer opportunity to take Aquinas scholar Brian Davies's course, "Introduction to St. Thomas Aquinas," at Fordham University, in the spring of 2001.

10. The late Jerry Garcia, band leader of the Grateful Dead, was singer on "I Know You Rider."

11. McDermott, *Summa: Concise Translation*, 181.

12. An example of "too tepid" an attachment would be a meager appetite for justice––the opposite of Matt. 5:6.

13. McDermott, 181.
14. McDermott, 181.
15. 1 Cor. 15:26.

X.

John Charles Henry

That Wide

January 5, 1954–February 25, 2016

If I say, "Surely the darkness will cover me,
and the light around me turn to night,"

Darkness is not dark to you;
the night is as bright as the day;
darkness and light to you are both alike.[1]

I will start with a word to my generation: we who grew up with Charles in this city. (He was by a year, less a day, my senior.) Ours was the Little Rock era when Hall High School reigned; when some of us were bussed to Central; when the Central–Hall Thanksgiving Day game felt like the Cotton Bowl and Arkansas–Texas felt like Armageddon; when all feared Father Tribou and Mama Lou;[2] when at the Razorback Twin, and on the sandbar, good times were plentiful;[3] when boys threw paper routes and girls might iron their hair; when in summertime we learned to waterski, then slalom, then ski double, sometimes triple, slicing back and forth across the wake and going airborne, until wiping out to cheers, laughter, and applause. Then we finished school, left home, grew up, and lived. That was our generation. Last Thursday afternoon, we lost one of the best and brightest of our place and time.

Next, I have a word for Dr. Henry's professional associates: you physicians, nurses, and others of the medical community who have come from near and far to pay your respects this morning. Welcome to this Cathedral. I hope you realize how much you mean to us. When we are broken, or wearing out, you do what you can to put things right or, failing that, to help us cope. We love you for that. Many here this morning loved Dr. Henry for that. God bless him and you for the life you shared and the work you've done together.

Now I speak to Charles's family, especially his children, beginning with a truth I pray is obvious and deeply felt. A bad end does not a bad life make. Your dad was a magnificent father. He wasn't good—he was great.

In counting the ways, let's start with fire. He loved to entrance and entertain you with it—finding the sweet spot for reward and risk, though giving risk the benefit of every doubt to wring out that extra dollop of enjoyment: fireworks on the Fourth, no holds barred; giant January bonfires on the Little Maumelle River, fueled by exploding Christmas trees; fire-lit paper Chinese lanterns slowly rising by the dozens up through summer darkness from Lake Ouachita. In baptism, we ask God for "the gift of joy and wonder in all your works."[4] In your dad that prayer was answered yes.

Now let's talk intelligence. Your father had it, and swept you up into his love of learning, giving credit both to logic and imagination. A motto familiar to his Hall High generation was: "A mind is a terrible thing to waste."[5] His wasn't wasted. Who else in the history of our state ever took the LSAT just to practice for the MCAT? His curiosity was lifelong, broad and eclectic, ranging from *The Basque History of the World* to the physics of potato guns. For this love of learning we should credit his college, Southwestern at Memphis—now called Rhodes, regrettably in my opinion. (That was me disliking change). In this corner of the south, Southwestern and Hendrix stood for learning as an end worthy in its own right.[6] In *The Idea of the University*, John Henry

Newman describes this liberal arts ideal: "A habit of mind is formed which lasts through life, of which the attributes are, freedom, equitableness, calmness, moderation, and wisdom." Newman calls it "a philosophical habit."[7] True to his school, your father had it, owned it, enjoyed it, and shared it with his children. Now it is yours to keep. Southwestern was also where he met and courted a Texarkana freshman who was the best thing to happen in his life: your mom.

> If I say, "Surely the darkness will cover me,
>   and the light around me turn to night,"
>
> Darkness is not dark to you;
> the night is as bright as the day;
>   darkness and light to you are both alike.[1]

Now a word to Christians, we of what is sometimes called "the faith community"—which is a ridiculous description. The communities on earth are very few and far between that do not operate from faith of one kind or another. What sets church apart is not that it has faith as such, but the shape and substance of the faith it has. Christ is the shape and substance of it. This room surrounds us with its sounds and imagery—though in a style, let's face it, that was a little over-rich at times to Charles's taste. He had been raised Presbyterian. In my long experience with Presbyterian men whose wives have coaxed them into becoming Episcopalians, there usually remains a residual preference for Calvinistic austerity. Privately, they still think Episcopalians, with our fancy vestments, bells, and smoke or whatnot, are the girl who spreads on too much rouge and lipstick. Beneath differences of style, however, there is deep agreement as to shape and substance.

As Christians, what are we to make of Charles's life—bad end now included? Charles confessed to someone recently that he felt like an imposter. I think we all know that deflated feeling. Feeling so doesn't mean we are that. Just turn the thought around and use a little logic. Sometimes our self-image is inflated. We think we're bigger and better than we are. In those moments we are the "proud in the imagination of their hearts" that God scatters in the *Magnificat*.[8] If our feeling that we're special doesn't make it so, neither would our thinking that we're worthless. Charles was no imposter, and I know that because the love he gave, with fire and learning, to his family, is manifestly real. The Bible supplies the yardstick for measuring spiritual authenticity. It is not self-image. It is fruit. By its fruits you shall know the vine, said the Lord.[9] By that measure, Charles Henry's life was bountiful.

Now what of his death?

These days, we are naturally inclined to take a medical, rather than a moral, view of suicide. When we hear of it, we ask about depression. That is wisdom from experience, because almost every time it is a potent factor. But we cannot let that explanation stand as though it were alone sufficient. That makes us puppets of our neurochemistry. And that is an insult, both to humanity and to Charles's education. The "liberal" in "liberal arts" is from the Latin *liber*, which means free. Charles did not believe he was a puppet, and I don't believe it either. And there's the rub. To the extent that we are free to choose our path, we find the moral question on the table. I'll say something obvious again: Charles could have done much better than he did on Thursday, and for the love of Christ, his wife and children, and himself, he should have.

An old teaching about sin holds that it comes in three kinds: sins of ignorance, sins of weakness, and sins of malice. Ignorance is when I know not what I do. Weakness is when I know and want to do what's best, but some other impulse gets the better of me and I fail. Malice is when I mean to hurt another creature for the pleasure of it. Malice is poison and there is no place for it in heaven. But save for the sometime ignorant and weak, heaven would be almost empty. Last Sunday in church we sang a hymn that feels more Methodist than either Presbyterian or Episcopalian, and glorifies the truth that all of us depend on:

> There's a wideness in God's mercy like the wideness of the sea.[10]

Wide as the Pacific is the mercy of the Lord. That is the faith of this community, and in that faith, we need not worry for our friend.

> If I say, "Surely the darkness will cover me,
>   and the light around me turn to night,"
>
> Darkness is not dark to you;
> the night is as bright as the day;
>   darkness and light to you are both alike.[1]

Thursday was a black day, and it will cast a shadow. With time, the shadow's hue will soften, its grip will slacken, and its compass will shrink. Today it looms ominous: large, intense, and dark. It is Good Friday. Dark means incomprehensible—we cannot really understand this— and it means painful. Charles's death confuses us, and it is more than faith can bear—except the faith that calls that Friday "Good."

In this faith, we know the good of a generation, a profession, and a family is not lost. Darkness is not dark to God. Evil is no match for Christ. We trust this heart and soul. We bind it to our prayers. We believe it for the love of Christ. We own it for ourselves, and for each other, and for Charles, this dear good man, our friend. May he dwell forever with the saints in light.

Notes

1. Psalm 139:10–11, Book of Common Prayer, 794.

2. Father George Tribou was the revered, old-school, tough-love principal of Catholic High School. We public school fellows gave him a wide berth. "Mama Lou's" was a creaky, long-abandoned building in the boondocks—haunted by unhappy spirits, as the story went. We would go there in small groups on dark nights, with flashlights, and see who was brave enough to make it to the second floor.

3. The Razorback Twin was a landmark two-screen drive-in movie theater, with giant red hogs emblazoned on the backsides of the facing screens. The "sandbar" was a vast, white-sand river beach, with scrubby trees and brush for hiding love and mischief, before the Arkansas River was tamed by Parks and Recreation and the Corps of Engineers.

4. "Holy Baptism," Book of Common Prayer, 308.

5. This was the perfect motto of the United Negro College Fund, *circa* 1972.

6. Hendrix College is in Conway, Arkansas.

7. John Henry Newman, *The Idea of a University Defined and Illustrated: In Nine Discourses Delivered to the Catholics of Dublin* (A Public Domain Book, 1852) location 1554 of 7431, Kindle.

8. Luke 1:51 (KJV).

9. A conflation of Matt. 7:20 and John 15:1–6.

10. "There's a Wideness in God's Mercy," The Hymnal 1982, Hymn 470.

XI.

Phyllis Anne Raney

Ghost Story

July 24, 1931–April 2, 2019

The Lord Jesus on the night when he was betrayed took a loaf of bread, and when he had given thanks, he broke it and said, "This is my body that is for you. Do this in remembrance of me." In the same way he took the cup also, after supper, saying, "This cup is the new covenant in my blood. Do this, as often as you drink it, in remembrance of me."[1]

That was St. Paul, from his first letter to the Corinthians. Scholars calculate that letter to have been written in "late winter or early spring," 55 AD.[2] The occasion it reports, the last supper, had taken place twenty-two years earlier at the same time of year. When a story about something is written during the lifetime of a witness to the original event, we say it was written within "living memory." That period can stretch to more than eighty years. Most if not all of the New Testament was written within living memory of Jesus.

Concerning Phyllis, I am going to start by telling a story of something that happened, involving her, not quite a quarter century ago. It is easily in living memory. I wrote it, I remember it, and I am still here. So is one of the two central original participants, the other being Phyllis. The story begins at a celebration of the Holy Eucharist. The Eucharist is how the last supper lives in *sacred* memory, which it will do forever.

One Sunday morning at St. Margaret's Church, Janie McDonald arrived early to prepare the flowers for the altar. I use the term altar loosely. St. Margaret's was meeting at that time at Cinema City, Breckenridge Village, where our altar consisted of a standard folding table suspended on a board raised on packing crates and covered by a bedspread.[3] Janie stood by while the altar crew put the thing together. No one knew it, but Janie was in a grim state. She was in pain, upset, and frightened. The date was October 22, 1995. Janie had dreaded that day for years.

This has to do with Janie and her father, David. Janie and her father shared a birthday—September 22. Imagine how special it had been for David McDonald to hold his newborn daughter on his own birthday. It was pure delight for Janie growing up, making birthday wishes and blowing out candles side by side with her dad. That picture is emblematic, because they were just that close in almost every way. Janie was David's spitting image, everybody said, and the apple of his eye, which suited him and her just fine. They seemed to feel and think in sync. In Stuttgart, Arkansas, all knew Janie as her daddy's girl.

On October 22, 1968, David McDonald committed suicide. Janie's age that day and his felt symbiotic: she was 14 and her father 41.

On September 22, 1995, Janie had arrived at forty-one. A countdown started. October 22 would be the day she reached the age her father took his life. How would she feel? What would she think? What would she do? It was a Sunday, so she came to church. She prepared the flowers, because she had been assigned. That done, she took her seat for worship. Episcopalians know the rhythm: Sing, pray, sing, listen. Sing, listen, pray, sing. Pray, come forward for communion. At the theater, we received communion standing. Lines formed up both aisles. You would come forward, hands extended, to receive the bread, then step to the right to take the cup. I was serving bread at Janie's aisle. Phyllis was at my side that day, administering the chalice. Neither of us had any inkling of Janie's state of mind. Janie took the bread, "The Body of Christ, the bread of heaven." Janie said "Amen" and stepped aside and turned to take the cup. Phyllis said the words: "The Blood of Christ, the cup of salvation."

Wine flew all over Janie.

I didn't see it happen. Neither Phyllis nor Janie could say how it happened. Phyllis recalled that her cup was getting low. She had scanned about for an acolyte to top it off. Janie had reached to take the cup. Before she knew it, she'd been splashed. Wine dripped from her face and hair, soaked her dress, and stained her shoes. Phyllis was mortified. She bent to try to wipe the wine from Janie's shoes. Janie turned away in horror. This wine was blood.[4] She had come to church distressed. She went home in trauma.

Early the next morning, Janie received a call from Jane. Jane Hunt had been Janie McDonald's best friend growing up in Stuttgart, who had walked with her through the devastation of her father's death. Jane was calling now because she'd had an awful dream of Janie. Janie's hair had always been conspicuously blond. It was her trademark. In Jane's nightmare, Janie's hair turned black. Jane woke up alarmed. She would check on Janie. *Jane*: "Janie, are you all right?" *Janie*: "No, I'm not." She told Jane what had happened at church. Janie felt she was about to fall apart.

Jane called me. I said bring her in.

Jane and Janie came together to my office, where Janie told me about her father, his suicide, her birthday, and the wine. Janie was shaken. Literally, she shook. For years, she had looked to this October 22 in fear that her sympathy for her father might drop her into a compulsion to follow in his footsteps. It was not only what he had done, but what she might do, that had put her in this state. She feared she was in the grip of something evil.

What did I make of that? Janie tells me I was reassuring. I guessed she would not go so far as to take her life to complete a mystic loop. But of course I was concerned. Her distress and fear called for serious attention. I wanted her to "see someone." "Who?" she asked. "Phyllis Raney" I said—who had held the cup from which the wine had spilled. Phyllis was often my first suggestion for counseling referrals. Whether I saw a further reason for suggesting Phyllis in what happened with the cup, I can't recall. Probably, I did.

Janie agreed to call Phyllis that morning and find when Phyllis might be available to see her. Janie called. Phyllis picked up. Coincidentally, a client had only just telephoned to cancel for that afternoon. See you at three o'clock.

Janie arrives at Phyllis's office. Come in, sit down, may I get you a glass of tea, no thank you. Janie opens up and pours out. She tells Phyllis about her father, about their birthday, about their closeness, and about the tempest in her heart and mind as she had come to church the day before. October 22 was her day of infamy.

Phyllis went to goosebumps. She lost detachment. To Janie's complete surprise, Phyllis interrupted her and began to talk about herself. Phyllis told Janie about her own life, and her own father. Phyllis's natural father had died when Phyllis was a baby. Her mother had then married Edward Peters, who would be to her a kind and loving husband and, to Phyllis, a devoted dad. Ed was the man Phyllis truly knew and loved as father. Phyllis went on about how close they were and how much she missed him. Janie listened and wondered: Why are you telling me this? Then Phyllis told her. Phyllis, too, had come to church distracted yesterday. Her heart, too, was troubled, as she administered the cup. She, too, had been thinking about her father. October 22 was the anniversary of Ed Peter's suicide.

In a dark room, someone had snapped the shade. Light poured in.

I will finish that story in a moment.

If I were to rank my all time list of fun parishioners, Phyllis would easily make the final four, while also being among the most faithful. For decades, I sent people to Phyllis for counsel. We cotaught classes on marriage. To clients and friends in trouble, she was wise and gracious. As to politics, she was more conservative than your average shrink. As to dinner conversation, she was a laugh a minute—unless you were her chef or waiter. For them, satisfying Phyllis was—this is her funeral, so I will opt for understatement—an uphill climb. Come Sunday morning, Phyllis would not be deterred from attending church and partaking of communion. Bad cancer was not near enough reason to make her miss. She came, she prayed, she stayed for class, and she paid close attention. Some years ago, before I came as dean, I received an email from Phyllis with a question about the resurrection. In a Sunday adult formation class, the leader had minimized its importance, and perhaps had disavowed it, except as metaphor for spiritual renewal. Phyllis didn't like that and wanted to know what I thought. She knew me and was not surprised when I got on my soapbox. Like the Declaration of Independence matters to the birth of the American republic, to Christian faith the resurrection matters. If Christ was not raised, and I mean it literally, our faith in God has entirely missed the mark. The goodness of God is thrown back into doubt and so is God's power to deliver us from sin and evil. The doctrines and practices of Christian faith are not isolated silos, each independent of the others. They are instead a web of intricate connections.

Remove the resurrection and the web dissolves. St. Paul had that in mind when he declared: "If for this life only we have hoped in Christ," we Christians are pathetic.[5] Phyllis had heard that speech before and liked it, which was why it had been me she'd asked.

Back to our story.

One day, Janie McDonald asked me what I thought about the wine. I took her to mean how would I explain it, the wine leaving the chalice in Phyllis's hand and splashing her that quarter century ago. I put it this way. Let's take the date, the wine, the dream, the cancelled appointment, and the bond these women through this series of events discovered. Let's consider the result. Janie, joined by Phyllis, was lifted from despair to wonder. For both women, October 22 had taken on a second meaning that, to say the least, hints strongly of redemption.

What do I make of that?

As Jesus' death drew near he made a promise:

I will not leave you orphaned; I am coming to you. In a little while the world will no longer see me, but you will see me. . . . Those who love me will keep my word, and my Father will love them, and we will come to them and make our home with them.[6]

"We will come to them and make our home with them." God and Christ at home in those who love and follow him—this is the promise of the Holy Spirit.

What do I think?

I think I have told a ghost story that happens to be true. Its ghost is the Spirit from on High, who had come as promised and made our new church a home. As in the movie, we built it and he came.[7]

This week, Tuesday morning, I went by to see Phyllis in the hospice unit at St. Vincent's. As I left the room, I called Janie who had been wanting to come and see her friend. "Janie, this is Chris. I think it's time." Janie was in Stuttgart attending to her mother, who was ill.[8] About two hours later, my phone rang. It was Janie calling me. She had rushed back to Little Rock and was now with Phyllis and a hospice chaplain bedside. Phyllis's breaths had stopped. The chaplain had called the nurse. The nurse had checked her pulse. The end had come.

Notes

1. 1 Cor. 11:23–25.

2. *The Interpreter's Dictionary of the Bible* (Nashville: Abingdon, 1962), s.v. "Corinthians, First Letter."

3. St. Margaret's Episcopal Church, in Little Rock, began holding services at Market Street Bargain Cinema on November 3, 1991, and moved twice: first to Cinema City for a larger space, and then to its new facilities in 1995. I was the vicar and Phyllis was among a core of "missionary members," sent out from other parishes, to help start and grow the new congregation. Later, she would return to her sending parish, Trinity Cathedral, from whence she was buried while I was dean.

4. "This wine was blood." Episcopalians believe we receive the blood of Christ in the sacramental wine. In my religion-science work, I saw this belief disparaged by Daniel Dennett, the philosopher, with a suggestion that it could be proved or disproved by sending the sacramental wine to a lab "to see if there was hemoglobin in it." Actually, a taste test should be enough to assure Professor Dennett that his suspicion is correct—the liquid in the cup is chemically still wine. Or, he might have consulted Thomas Aquinas, who would have told him the same thing. "That this sacrament contains the actual body and blood of Christ cannot be perceived with our senses but only by faith in God's authority." What we *can* see, as Aquinas goes on to say, is that it is "appropriate" that the sacrament convey Christ's blood and body. By this Aquinas means that we can see how this sacrament fits faith's need in several ways. For example, it makes Christ present on our journey (we need not walk alone); and it makes his presence sensible in a human-friendly form (the pleasing taste of bread and wine); and it is a reasonable belief, given what we know of God. On this last point, here is something worth remembering: given the love of God, many wonderful things make sense that would be otherwise farfetched. See Daniel C. Dennett, *Breaking the Spell: Religion as a Natural Phenomenon* (New York: Viking, 2006), 227; Mc-

Dermott, *Summa: Concise Translation*, 570–71; Aquinas, ST part three, question 73, "The Eucharist," article 5, corpus.

5. 1 Cor. 15:19.

6. John 14:18–19, 23.

7. "If you build it, he will come," from *Field of Dreams*.

8. Stuttgart, Arkansas, "The Duck Capitol of the World," is an hour's drive from Little Rock.

XII.

James Julian Schreiber

In the Power of the Spirit

January 14, 1992–March 7, 2020

There is one Body and one Spirit;
There is one hope in God's call to us;
One Lord, one Faith, one Baptism;
One God and Father of all.[1]

That call and response announces our baptismal service in the Book of Common Prayer. It echoes here this morning, because this is not the first time Cindy and Richard have presented their beloved son to God at St. Margaret's altar. As some of you remember, the altar the first time was a makeshift apparatus covered by a holy-looking bedspread—the best we could do at the Market Street Bargain Cinema, where we met for worship at the time. The day was Sunday, January 10, 1993. The font then was the same as now—a legacy from St. Michael's, Arkadelphia. You pass it every Sunday morning walking in. That January Sunday, James Julian, handsome in white, was happy in his mother's arms.

As Officiant, I would ask the ancient questions. As parents, Cindy and Richard, with other sponsors, would answer for their son.[2] For example:

Question   Do you renounce Satan and the spiritual forces of wickedness that rebel against God?
Answer   I renounce them.

That was no trouble, because JJ Schreiber grew up the

natural opposite of wicked. He was devoid of malice, as gentle a child and kind a man as one could hope to know. "I love you so very much," he would always say, sincerely, to his mom when signing off from phone calls. At my desk in an office adjoining Cindy's, I often overheard that signoff more than once a day. At Cindy's feet, another gentle soul named Phydeaux, the Fribourgh-Schreibers' standard poodle, would listen in approvingly. Remember Phydeaux. We'll come back to him.

> *Question* Do you renounce the evil powers of this world which corrupt and destroy the creatures of God?
> *Answer* I renounce them.

That turns out to be the tall order. Malice is typically a man-sized problem, but evil is world-sized and multifaceted. The COVID pandemic illustrates the point, as do the drug trade and opioid addiction epidemic.[3] Evil, Thomas Aquinas taught us, is not a presence but an absence: the *privatio boni*—absence of the good.[4] By no means is that to minimize its powers, which infiltrate, take root, and spread with tragic impact. "I renounce them," JJ's parents bravely said, who would be valiant for their son in fighting them.

Let's talk about dogs.

I just put down a novel whose story is partly told as seen by an Ozark Mountain cur dog. Once I got started and knew what I had, I read the book as slowly as I could to make it last. One of the perks of Arkansas life is exposure to its writer, Donald Harington, whom no one much from anywhere else has heard of. It is their loss, although it may be that you need to spend some extra time here to appreciate his take on Arkansas. He sees beauty in our little Ozarks absent elsewhere—a privatio beauty. He writes that California, for example, "for all its fabled splendors, was simply no match" for a certain Newton County mountaintop and gorge.[5] Probably, your average west or east coast reader can't relate to that. Uniquely, that is our Arkie privilege.

The novel, titled *With*, begins: "She tried to run away." It took three pages for me to catch on that "she" walks on four legs and enjoys a good bone. For chapter one, at least, we are seeing life as dogs do. We learn our dog-friend's name is Hreapha, and that it was given to her by her mother. Her master, who doesn't know this, calls her "Bitch." In this man the spiritual forces of wickedness are comfortably at home. Hreapha knows this all too well to her chagrin. "Bad Man," she barked, that time she tried to run away.[6] But usually she minds him, and not only from fear of getting whipped or cussed. She is a good dog and loyalty is in her blood.

This brings us back to Phydeaux. Phydeaux Fribourgh-Schreiber loved his brother JJ with concern and care, but never judgment. In this way, dogs are more like God than we are. In Genesis, we read that God made the heavens and the earth, and all creatures great and small, and "God saw that it was good."[7] In his *Summa Theologiae*, Aquinas picks up that theme and runs with it.[8] Each fragment of the created whole is good in its own way, and in that way expresses goodness at its source in God. So every poodle, piece of quartz, and maple leaf has its ways of being god-like. We people have them too, including some that other creatures don't. By the same token, other creatures possess goodness that we lack. To sense the goodness of God's loyalty to JJ, consider Phydeaux.

Happily, Hreapha's creepy master is eventually displaced by Robin, a young mistress worthy of her loyalty and love. Minding Robin is both duty and delight. For dogs, we learn, "minding" means much more than doing what they're told.

Hreapha's mentor (who goes by the name of Yowrfrowr) gives human readers a tutorial. Yes, minding is doing: sit, fetch, stay, and whatnot. But it is knowing too. Sounding a little like Aquinas, Yowrfrowr defines his term. Minding is "the faculty of knowing what is in one's master's mind."[9] Hreapha's faculty is extra sharp, easily minding what Robin needs, wants and, to the extent a mountain cur can fathom teenage human cogitation, even what she's thinking. How does she mind? In the novel, extrasensory perception happens once or twice, but ESP is not a way of knowing man or dog can count on. Hreapha's methods are forensic. She knows what she gleans from what she sees, hears, tastes, smells, or touches. "You can't very well mind something you can't see," she says.[10]

Tuesday morning by text I asked Cindy if she knew the date JJ was baptized. She did and sent back: January 10, 1993. Suddenly and simultaneously, both of us were typing the same thought. "That was the First Sunday after the Epiphany." By a second or so, her message reached me first. Throughout the season of Epiphany, seeing's part in knowing is the theme. Christ is God made visible to flesh and blood, so that, to the extent that human folk are able, we can know God's mind. "We have the mind of Christ," Paul says.[11]

With her Tuesday text, Cindy included a photo of a memento from the service. Seeing it, I smiled. It was a picture of our home-cooked weekly service insert. For visitors unfamiliar with Episcopal beliefs and ways, the insert would typically include a little written piece, locally produced by us, explaining something in the service. The entry for that January 10 was titled: "Baptizing Infants." It posed the old question: "Some honorable Christians will not baptize those who cannot believe and speak for themselves. Why then do we?" This was our answer:

The late Archbishop of Canterbury, William Temple, was once approached by a man who asked 'Brother, are you saved?' 'Yes,' he replied, 'two thousand years ago on Calvary.' The crux of the matter is this: Our church understands baptism as a sign (sacrament) of something that happens for us, rather than of something that happens within us. Neither the six-week-old babe in arms nor the eighty-year-old stroke victim in coma is capable of belief in their salvation. Nevertheless, as part of the Christian Church, they may stand among those who bear the sign of the love of God for them in Christ, which is given to them in baptism.

In the insert, I saw that we sang "Hymn 296." I looked it up, absorbed the first two lines, and thought: "Spot on." "We know that Christ is raised and dies no more / Embraced by death he broke its fearful hold." Concerning death, we know God's mind. It is something we can fathom. God's son who died is raised and dies no more. He delivers us from evil. Yes, those forces we renounce are powerful. And he is more.

James Julian, beloved son, has died too young.

There is one Body and one Spirit;
There is one hope in God's call to us;
One Lord, one Faith, one Baptism;
One God and Father of all.

At the font that January 10th, I posed the second set of ancient questions:

Question   Do you turn to Jesus Christ and accept him as your savior?

(To JJ's Parents)   Twenty-seven years ago you said: "I do." Is that still your answer?[1]

Question   Do you put your whole trust in his grace and love?[1]

(To the congregation)   Cindy and Richard do. For the love of Christ and JJ, shall we join them?[3]

Question   Do you promise to follow and obey him as your Lord?[4]

Life teems with would-be lords and masters, bad and good. JJ has been delivered from a cruel one, by the sight of One worthy of his loyalty and love.

Do you remember?

It was first the water:

James Julian I baptize you in the name of the Father, and of the Son, and of the Holy Spirit. Amen.

Then the oil:

James Julian you are sealed by the Holy Spirit in baptism and marked as Christ's own forever. Amen.

He promises:

Anyone who comes to me I will never drive away.[12]

Amen. Amen. Amen.

---

1 Coming from a deep place, their reply in unison was "Yes."

2 Richard and Cindy, visibly moved, again said "Yes."

3 Nods were seen and yesses heard throughout the church.

4 "We do," they said, in the power of the Spirit.

Notes

1. "Holy Baptism," Book of Common Prayer, 299.

2. Richard Schreiber, JJ's father, was also baptized at St. Margaret's. Cindy Fribourgh, Richard's wife and JJ's mother, was one of St. Margaret's early senior wardens and later was ordained deacon. Since 2011, Cindy and I have worked in tandem as cofounders and leaders of SUMMA, a high school theological debate program of the University of the South in Sewanee, Tennessee.

3. St. Margaret's was packed for the funeral on Thursday, March 12, 2020, one day after the first Arkansas coronavirus case popped up on the radar. It would be the last in-person worship service at St. Margaret's, and perhaps of any church in Little Rock, for months.

4. For Aquinas on evil, see: Davies, *The Thought of Thomas Aquinas*, 89–97.

5. Donald Harington, *With*, (Mildred CT: Toby Press, 2004), 322.

6. Harington, *With*, 3–10.

7. Gen. 1:1–31.

8. For Aquinas on goodness, see: Davies, 80–89.

9. Harington, *With*, 155.

10. Harington, *With*, 469.

11. 1 Cor 2:16.

12. John 6:37.

About the Author

Christoph Keller, III is an Episcopal priest and theologian. Born in El Dorado, Arkansas, he grew up in Arkansas and Mississippi. A 1977 graduate of Amherst College, he holds a doctorate (ThD) in Anglican Studies from General Theological Seminary in New York, where his field of emphasis was theology and science. His dissertation, "Darwin's Science in Chalcedonian Imagination," defends and explains compatibility between Christian faith and natural evolution. In 2012, he started SUMMA: A Student Theological Debate Society, with forty-seven high school students from central Arkansas. SUMMA, whose theme is "speaking truth in love," is now a summer program of the University of the South in Sewanee, TN, drawing students from around the world. As a pastor, he has served churches in Pine Bluff, Fort Smith, and Van Buren, Arkansas. In 1991, he started Little Rock's St. Margaret's Church, which initially met in a bargain cinema. From 2014 to 2020, he served as dean and rector of Little Rock's Trinity Cathedral--on the front steps of which he had met his wife, Julie, in 1967. Christoph and Julie have two grown children, and a third generation—all girls, so far--is rising up in strength. *Getting On Toward Home: And Other Sermons by the River* is his first book.

Further Praise

"Christoph Keller, III has mastered the formula for combining mind and heart into what he composes. This is especially true of his funeral sermons, where the heart almost always takes the lead through his homiletic journeys toward resurrection. Keller writes about a dear young man he baptized as an infant who died an early death. He has homilies for both of his well-known parents. He writes about beloved parishioners. He presides over the funeral of a talented physician who committed suicide. He preaches on the death of someone he has known since childhood. . . . Keller's funeral sermons simply best represent Frederick Buechner's description of preaching in *Telling Secrets*. 'It is to try to put the Gospel into words not the way you would compose an essay but the way you would write a poem or a love letter—putting your heart into it, your own excitement, most of all your whole life.'"

—*The Rev. Joanna Seibert, MD, deacon and author*

CPSIA information can be obtained
at www.ICGtesting.com
Printed in the USA
LVHW010923021121
702225LV00007B/228